HONDA

250 & 360cc TWINS • 1974-1977

SERVICE • REPAIR • PERFORMANCE

By

RAY HOY

ERIC JORGENSEN
Editor

JEFF ROBINSON
Publisher

CLYMER PUBLICATIONS

World's largest publisher of books devoted exclusively to
automobiles and motorcycles.

12860 MUSCATINE STREET • P.O. BOX 20 • ARLETA, CALIFORNIA 91331

FIRST EDITION
First Printing April, 1978
Second Printing July, 1978
Third Printing May, 1979

Printed in U.S.A.

ISBN: 0-89287-210-1

Performance Improvement chapter by Chris Bunch

•

Cover photo by Mike Brown — Visual Imagery, Los Angeles, California

CONTENTS

HONDA

250 & 360cc TWINS • 1974-1977

SERVICE • REPAIR • PERFORMANCE

QUICK REFERENCE DATA

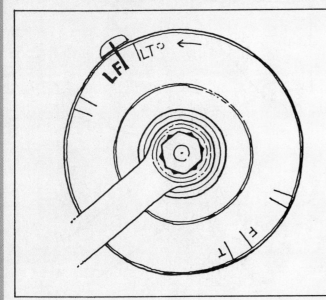

IGNITION TIMING

The "LF" mark on the alternator rotor must align with the index pointer just as the left-hand ignition breaker points begin to open. The right-hand ignition breaker points should just begin to open as the "F" mark and index pointer align.

TUNE-UP SPECIFICATIONS AND CAPACITIES

Breaker point gap	0.025-0.028 in. (0.60-0.70mm)
Spark plug gap	0.025-0.028 in. (0.60-0.70mm)
Valve clearance*	
Intake	0.002 in. (0.05mm)
Exhaust	0.003 in. (0.08mm)
Carburetor float height	0.75 in. (19.0mm)
Engine oil quantity	3.2 pints (1.5 liters)
Fork oil quantity	5.4-5.6 oz. (160-165cc)

* Valve clearance should be checked with engine cold.

ENGINE OIL GRADE

Temperature Range	Oil Viscosity
Below 32°F	10W, 10W-30, or 10W-40
32 to 60°F	20W, 10W-30, or 10W-40
Above 60°F	30W, 10W-30, or 10W-40

ADJUSTMENTS

Adjustment	Measurement
Drive chain play	3/4-1 in. (20-25mm)
Front brake lever free play	3/16-5/16 in. (5-8mm)
Rear brake pedal free play	3/4-1 in. (20-25mm)
Clutch lever free play	3/4 in. (20mm)

TIRES

Tire Size	Inflation Pressure (psi)
2.50-18	23
2.75-18	23
3.00-18	23
3.25-18	23
3.50-18	23
4.00-19	23
3.00-19	23
3.25-19	23

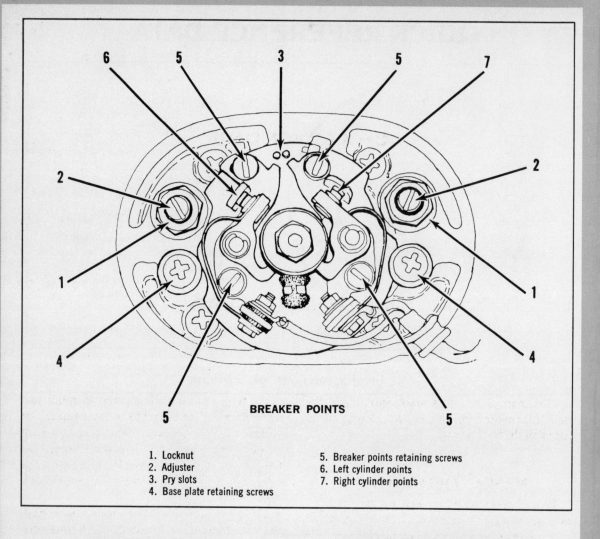

BREAKER POINTS

1. Locknut
2. Adjuster
3. Pry slots
4. Base plate retaining screws
5. Breaker points retaining screws
6. Left cylinder points
7. Right cylinder points

MAINTENANCE SCHEDULE

Maintenance Item	Miles 1,000	3,000	6,000
Engine tune-up		X	
Check battery	X		
Change oil	X	X	X
Service oil filter			X
Adjust clutch		X	
Check lights and horn	X		
Adjust chain	X		
Adjust brakes	X		
Check brake lining			X
Check wheels	X		
Check tires	X		
Change fork oil		X	
Grease wheel bearings			X
Check steering bearings			X
Grease swing arm		X	

IGNITION – NO SPARK/WEAK SPARK

Probable Cause	Remedy
• Discharged battery	Charge battery
• Defective fuse	Replace
• Defective main switch	Replace
• Loose or corroded connections	Clean and tighten
• Broken wire	Repair
• Incorrect point gap	Reset points. Be sure to readjust ignition timing
• Dirty or oily points	Clean points
• Spark plug lead damaged	Replace wire
• Broken primary wire	Repair wire
• Open winding in coil	Replace coil
• Shorted winding in coil	Replace coil
• Defective condenser	Replace condenser

CHAPTER ONE

GENERAL INFORMATION

This manual provides maintenance and repair information for all of the Honda twins listed on the back cover.

MANUAL ORGANIZATION

This chapter provides general information and discusses equipment and tools useful for preventive maintenance and troubleshooting.

Chapter Two explains lubrication and maintenance procedures necessary to keep your motorcycle running right, plus a complete tune-up section.

Chapter Three provides methods and suggestions for quick and accurate diagnosis and repair of problems. Troubleshooting procedures discuss typical symptoms and methods to pinpoint the trouble.

Chapter Four offers complete repair procedures for all Honda twin-cylinder engines.

Subsequent chapters describe specific systems such as fuel and exhaust systems; electrical system; and frame, suspension, and steering.

Each chapter provides disassembly, repair, and assembly procedures in simple step-by-step form. If a repair is impractical for a home mechanic, it is so indicated. It is usually faster and less expensive to take such repairs to a dealer or competent repair shop.

Throughout this manual keep in mind two conventions: "front" refers to the front of the motorcycle. The front of any component such as the engine is that end which faces toward the front of the motorcycle. The left and right sides refer to a person sitting on the motorcycle facing forward.

The terms NOTE, CAUTION, and WARNING have specific meanings in this manual. A NOTE provides additional information to make a step or procedure easier or clearer. Disregarding a NOTE could cause inconvenience, but would not cause damage or personal injury.

A CAUTION emphasizes areas where equipment damage could result. Disregarding a CAUTION could cause permanent mechanical damage; however, personal injury is unlikely.

A WARNING emphasizes areas where personal injury or even death could result from negligence. Mechanical damage may also occur. WARNINGS *are to be taken seriously*. In some cases serious injury or death has resulted from disregarding similar warnings.

The use of special tools has been kept to a minimum. Where special tools are required, illustrations are provided. The resourceful mechanic can, in many cases, improvise with acceptable substitutes—there is always another way. If a substitute is used, however, care should be exercised so as not to damage parts.

SERVICE HINTS

Most of the service procedures covered are straightforward and can be performed by anyone reasonably handy with tools. It is suggested, however, that you consider your own capabilities carefully before attempting any operation involving major disassembly of the engine.

Some operations, for example, require the use of a press. It would be wiser to have these performed by a shop equipped for such work, rather than trying to do the job yourself with makeshift equipment. Other procedures require precision measurements. Unless you have the skills and equipment to make these measurements, call on a competent service outlet.

You will find that repairs will go much faster and easier if your machine is clean before you begin work. There are special cleaners for washing the engine and related parts. You just brush or spray on the cleaning solution, let it stand, and rinse it away with a garden hose. Clean all oily or greasy parts with cleaning solvent as you remove them.

WARNING

Never use gasoline as a cleaning agent. Gasoline presents an extreme fire hazard. Be sure to work in a well-ventilated area when you use cleaning solvent of any kind. Keep a fire extinguisher handy, just in case.

Special tools are required for some service procedures. These tools may be purchased at Honda dealers. If you are on good terms with the dealer's service department, you may be able to use their tools.

Much of the labor charge for repairs made by dealers is for removal and disassembly of other parts in order to reach the defective one. It is frequently possible for you to do all of this yourself, then take the affected subassembly into the dealer for repair.

Once you decide to tackle the job yourself, read the engine section in this manual which pertains to the job. Study the illustrations and the text until you have a good idea of what is involved. If special tools are required, make arrangements to get them before you start the job. It is frustrating to get partly into a job and find that you are unable to complete it.

TOOLS

Every motorcyclist should carry a small tool kit with him, to help make minor roadside adjustments and repairs.

For more extensive servicing, an assortment of ordinary hand tools is required. As a minimum, have the following available.

  a. Combination wrenches (metric)
  b. Socket wrenches (metric)
  c. Assorted screwdrivers
  d. Assorted pliers
  e. Spark plug gauge
  f. Spark plug wrench
  g. Small hammer
  h. Plastic mallet
  i. Parts cleaning brush

A few special tools may also be required. The first four listed below are essential.

Ignition Gauge

This tool combines round wire spark plug gap gauges with narrow breaker point feeler gauges. The device costs about $3 at auto accessory stores. See **Figure 1**.

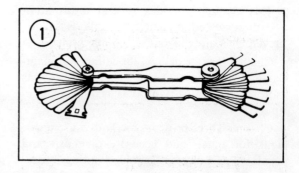

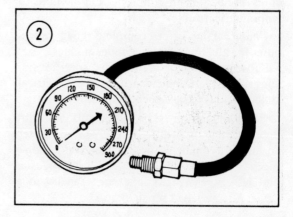

Compression Gauge

An engine with low compression cannot be properly tuned and will not develop full power. A compression gauge measures engine compression. The one shown in **Figure 2** has a flexible stem, which enables it to reach cylinders where there is little clearance between the cylinder head and frame. Inexpensive gauges start at around $3, and are available at auto accessory stores or by mail order.

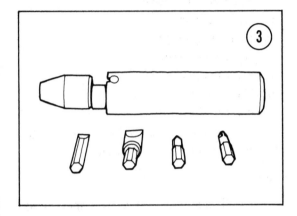

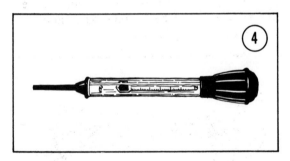

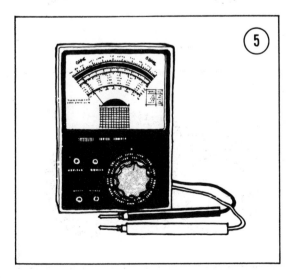

Impact Driver

This tool might have been designed with the motorcycle mechanic in mind. It makes removal of engine cover screws easy, and eliminates damaged screw slots. Good ones run about $12 at larger hardware stores. See **Figure 3**.

Hydrometer

This instrument measures state of charge of the battery, and tells much about battery condition. Such an instrument is available at any auto parts store and through most larger mail order outlets. Satisfactory ones cost as little as $3. See **Figure 4**.

Multimeter or VOM

This instrument is invaluable for electrical system troubleshooting and service. A few of its functions may be duplicated by locally fabricated substitutes, but for the serious hobbyist, it is a must. See **Figure 5**.

EXPENDABLE SUPPLIES

Certain expendable supplies are also required. These include grease, oil, gasket cement, wiping rags, cleaning solvent, and distilled water. Cleaning solvent is available at many service stations. Distilled water, required for battery service, is available at every supermarket.

MECHANIC'S TIPS

Removing Frozen Nuts and Screws

When a fastener rusts and cannot be removed, several methods may be used to loosen it. First apply penetrating oil liberally. Rap the fastener several times with a small hammer; don't hit it hard enough to cause damage.

For frozen screws, apply oil as described, then insert a screwdriver in the slot and rap the top of the screwdriver with a hammer. This loosens the rust so the screw can be removed in the normal way. If the screw head is too chewed up to use a screwdriver, grip the head with vise-type pliers and turn the screw out.

For a frozen bolt or nut, apply penetrating oil, then rap it with a hammer. Turn off with the proper size wrench. If the points are rounded off, grip with vise-type pliers as described for screws.

Stripped Threads

Occasionally, threads are stripped through carelessness or impact damage. Often the threads can be cleaned up by running a tap (for internal threads) or die (for external threads) through the threads. See **Figure 6**.

Broken Screw or Bolt

When the head breaks off a screw or bolt, several methods are available for removing the remaining portion.

If a large portion of the remainder projects out, try gripping it with vise-type pliers. If the projection portion is too small, try filing it to fit a wrench or cut a slot in it to fit a screwdriver. See **Figure 7**.

If the head breaks off flush, as it usually does, remove it with a screw extractor. Refer to **Figure 8**. Center-punch the broken part, then drill a hole into it. Drill sizes are marked on the tool. Tap the extractor into the broken part, then back it out with a wrench.

Removing Damaged Screws

WARNING
When removing screws by this method, always wear suitable eye protection.

CAUTION
Use clean rags to cover bearings or any other parts which might be harmed by metal chips produced during this procedure.

Figure 9 illustrates damaged screws typical of those on many bikes. Such screws may usually be removed easily by drilling. Select a bit with a diameter larger than that of the damaged screw, but smaller than its head, then drill into the screw head (**Figure 10**) until the head separates from the screw. The remainder of the screw may then be turned out easily. **Figure 11** illustrates one screw head removed in this man-

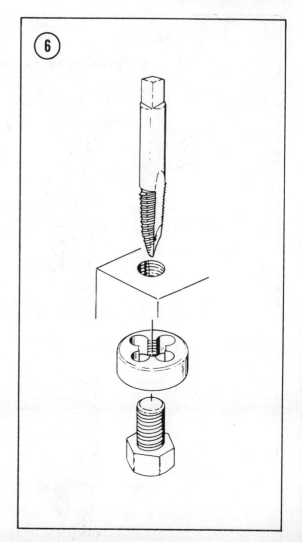

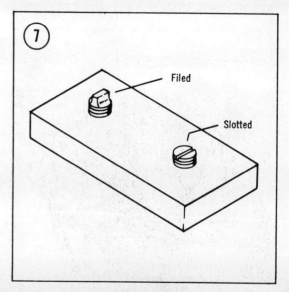

8

1

REMOVING BROKEN SCREWS AND BOLTS

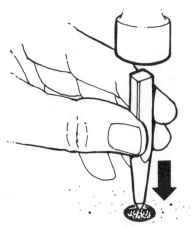

1. Center punch broken stud

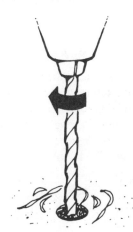

2. Drill hole in stud

3. Tap in screw extractor

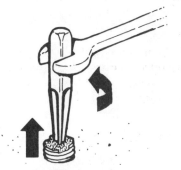

4. Remove broken stud

9

10

ner. The other has been drilled to just the point where the head is separating from the screw body. Note that there is no damage to the plate which these screws retain.

SAFETY FIRST

Professional mechanics can work for years without sustaining serious injury. If you observe a few rules of common sense and safety, you can also enjoy many safe hours servicing your own machine. You can also hurt yourself or damage the bike if you ignore these rules:

1. Never use gasoline as a cleaning solvent.

2. Never smoke or use a torch near flammable liquids, such as cleaning solvent in open containers.

3. Never smoke or use a torch in an area where batteries are charging. Highly explosive hydrogen gas is formed during the charging process.

4. If welding or brazing is required on the machine, remove the fuel tank to a safe distance, at least 50 feet away.

5. Be sure to use proper size wrenches for nut turning.

6. If a nut is tight, think for a moment what would happen to your hand should the wrench slip. Be guided accordingly.

7. Keep your work area clean and uncluttered.

8. Wear safety goggles in all operations involving drilling, grinding, or use of a chisel.

9. Never use worn tools.

10. Keep a fire extinguisher handy. Be sure that it is rated for gasoline and electrical fires.

CHAPTER TWO

2

LUBRICATION AND MAINTENANCE

To gain the utmost in safety, performance, and useful life from your motorcycle, it is necessary to make periodic inspections and adjustments. It frequently happens that minor problems found during such inspections are simple and inexpensive to correct at the time, but could lead to major failures later. This chapter describes such services.

Table 1 is a suggested maintenance schedule.

ENGINE TUNE-UP

The purpose of a tune-up is to restore power and performance lost over a gradual period of time due to normal wear.

Carry out the tune-up in the same sequence as in this chapter for best results.

Cam Chain Adjustment

Engine valves and breaker points are opened and closed by a chain-driven camshaft. Wear in this chain results in altered valve and ignition timing, so it is necessary to adjust chain tension periodically.

1. Remove alternator cover (**Figure 1**).

2. Place a wrench on the alternator rotor retaining nut and rotate engine counterclockwise until all valves are closed (this occurs when the LT mark on the rotor is 90 degrees past the in-

dex pointer). Refer to **Figure 2**. If valves are still open, continue to rotate engine another full turn.

3. Refer to **Figure 3**. Loosen locknut, then tensioner bolt. Chain slack will automatically be taken up by the tensioner mechanism.

4. Tighten and hold bolt with a wrench while you tighten locknut.

Table 1   MAINTENANCE SCHEDULE

Maintenance Item	1,000	Miles 3,000	6,000
Engine tune-up		X	
Check battery	X		
Change oil	X	X	X
Service oil filter			X
Adjust clutch		X	
Check lights and horn	X		
Adjust chain	X		
Adjust brakes	X		
Check brake lining			X
Check wheels	X		
Check tires	X		
Change fork oil		X	
Grease wheel bearings			X
Check steering bearings			X
Grease swing arm		X	

Valve Adjustment

Valves must be adjusted while the engine is cold.

1. Open seat and raise rear of fuel tank (**Figure 4**).

2. Remove alternator cover (refer to **Figure 1**).

3. Remove tappet covers (**Figure 5**).

4. Place a wrench on the alternator rotor bolt and turn engine counterclockwise until left cylinder intake valve opens fully, then starts to close. Continue turning engine from this point until LT mark on alternator rotor aligns with the index pointer (**Figure 6**). Note that both valves for the left cylinder are fully closed at this point.

5. Insert a feeler gauge between tappet adjuster screw and valve stem. The intake valve clearance should be 0.002 in. (0.05mm), and the exhaust valve clearance 0.003 in. (0.08mm).

6. If clearance is not correct, refer to **Figure 7**. Loosen locknut, then turn adjustment screw to produce a slight drag on the feeler gauge. Hold screw in position and tighten locknut.

> NOTE: *Clearance may change when locknut is tightened, so recheck adjustment and readjust if necessary.*

7. After both left cylinder valves are adjusted, turn engine counterclockwise (180 degrees) until T mark on rotor aligns with index. Adjust right cylinder valves (follow Steps 5 and 6, preceding).

Compression Test

An engine requires adequate compression to develop full power. If for any reason compression is low, the engine will not develop full power. A compression test, or even better, a series of them over the life of the motorcycle, will tell much about engine condition.

To carry out a compression test, proceed as follows:

1. Start the engine, then ride the bike long enough to warm it thoroughly.

2. Remove each spark plug (refer to *Spark Plug Inspection and Service,* following section).

3. Screw a compression gauge into the spark plug hole, or if a press-in type gauge is used, hold it firmly in position (**Figure 8**).

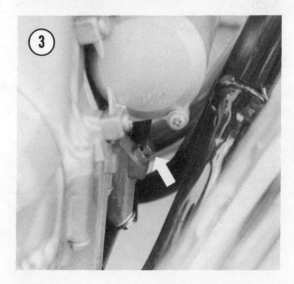

4. With the ignition switch OFF, and the throttle wide open, crank the engine briskly with the kickstarter several times; the compression gauge indication will increase with each kick. Continue to crank the engine until the gauge shows no more increase, then record the gauge indication. For example, on the first kick the gauge might indicate 90 psi; the second kick, 140 psi; the third kick, 160 psi, etc.

5. Repeat this procedure for the remaining cylinder. Normal compression pressure at sea level will be about 140-170 psi, decreasing with altitude.

A sudden drop in cylinder compression could be caused by many factors, most of which require major engine service. Some of these causes are worn piston rings, a leaking cylinder head gasket, or a leaking valve.

A quick check for worn piston rings is easy: pour a spoonful of heavy engine oil through the spark plug opening. The oil will flow over the

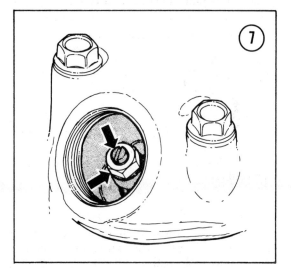

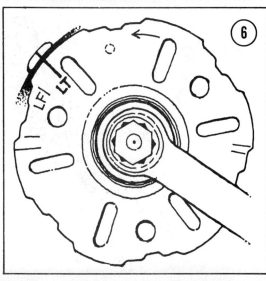

head of the piston, temporarily sealing the piston rings. Repeat the compression test for that cylinder. If compression comes up to normal (or near normal), it is an indication that the rings are worn, or the cylinder defective.

If compression remains low after pouring oil into the spark plug hole and repeating the compression test, it is likely that a valve or head gasket is leaking. (A rapid on-off squeal when the engine is running frequently accompanies this condition.)

On Honda twins, a difference of 25 percent in compression measurements between cylinders should be taken as an indication that engine repairs should be made. Likewise, a difference of 25 percent between successive measurements on any cylinder over a period of time (if made under identical conditions) is also an indication of trouble.

Table 2 may be used as a quick reference when checking cylinder compression pressures. It has been calculated so that the lowest reading number is 75 percent of the highest reading number.

Example: After checking the compression pressures in all cylinders it was found that the highest pressure obtained was 150 psi. The lowest pressure reading was 140 psi. By locating 150 in the maximum column, it is seen that the minimum allowable pressure is 113. Since the lowest reading obtained was 140 psi, the compression is within satisfactory limits.

**Spark Plug Inspection
and Service**

Spark plugs are available in various heat ranges hotter or colder than the spark plug originally installed at the factory.

Select plugs of a heat range designed for the loads and temperature conditions under which the engine will run. Use of incorrect heat ranges can cause seized pistons, scored cylinder walls, or damaged piston crowns.

In general, use a low-numbered plug for low speeds, low loads, and low temperatures. Use a higher-numbered plug for high speeds, high engine loads, and high temperatures.

NOTE: *Use the highest numbered plug that will not foul. In areas where*

seasonal temperature variations are great, the factory recommends using a high-numbered plug for slower winter operation.

The reach (length) of a plug is also important. A longer-than-normal plug could interfere with the piston, causing severe damage. Refer to **Figures 9 and 10**.

Spark plugs of the correct heat range, with the engine in a proper state of tune, will appear light tan. See **Figure 11** (page 12) for the various spark plug conditions you might encounter.

Changing spark plugs is generally a simple operation. Occasionally heat and corrosion can cause the plug to bind in the cylinder head, making removal difficult. Do not use force; the head is easily damaged. Here is the proper way to replace a plug.

1. Blow out any debris which has collected in the spark plug wells. It could fall into the hole and cause damage.

Table 2　COMPRESSION PRESSURE LIMITS

Pressure (psi)		Pressure (psi)	
Maximum	Minimum	Maximum	Minimum
134	101	188	141
136	102	190	142
138	104	192	144
140	105	194	145
142	107	196	147
146	110	198	148
148	111	200	150
150	113	202	151
152	114	204	153
154	115	206	154
156	117	208	156
158	118	210	157
160	120	212	158
162	121	214	160
164	123	216	162
166	124	218	163
168	126	220	165
170	127	222	166
172	129	224	168
174	131	226	169
176	132	228	171
178	133	230	172
180	135	232	174
182	136	234	175
184	138	236	177
186	140	238	178

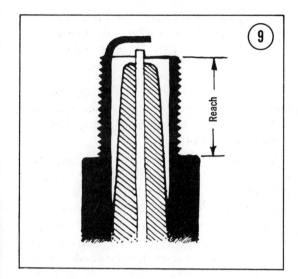

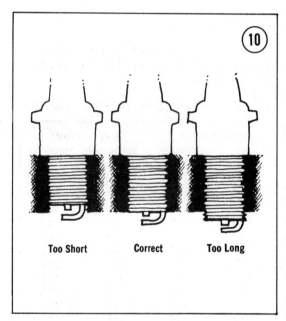

Too Short   Correct   Too Long

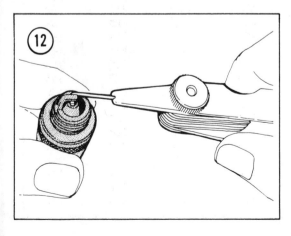

2. Gently remove the spark plug leads by pulling up and out on the cap. Do not jerk or pull on the wire itself.

3. Apply penetrating oil to the base of the plug and allow it to work into the threads.

4. Back out the plugs with a socket that has a rubber insert designed to grip the insulator. Be careful not to drop the plugs where they could become lodged.

NOTE: *Be sure that you remember which cylinder each spark plug came out of. The condition of the spark plug is an indication of engine condition and can warn of developing trouble that can be isolated by cylinder (refer to* **Figure 11**).

5. Remove the spark plug gaskets from the spark plug holes. Clean the seating area after removal, being careful that dirt does not drop into the spark plug hole.

6. Remove grease and dirt from the insulator with a clean rag. Inspect the insulator and body of each spark plug for signs of cracks and chips. Replace if defective.

NOTE: *If one plug is found unsatisfactory, replace both of them.*

7. Clean the tips of the plugs with a sandblasting machine (some gas stations have them) or a wire brush and solvent.

8. File the center electrode flat. Clean and file all surfaces of the outer electrode. All surfaces should be clean, flat, and smooth.

9. Use a round feeler gauge and adjust the clearance between the electrodes to 0.028-0.032 in. (0.70-0.80mm) for all models. See **Figure 12**.

CAUTION
Do not bend the inner electrode or damage to the insulator may result.

10. Use a new gasket if the old plugs are to be reused after cleaning. Apply a dab of graphite to the spark plug threads to simplify future removal.

11. Thread the plugs into the spark plug holes finger-tight, then tighten ¼ turn more with a wrench. Further tightening will flatten the gasket and cause binding. (If a torque wrench is available, tighten spark plugs to 15 ft.-lb.).

SPARK PLUG CONDITION

(11)

NORMAL
• Identified by light tan or gray deposits on the firing tip.
• Can be cleaned.

GAP BRIDGED
• Identified by deposit buildup closing gap between electrodes.
• Caused by oil or carbon fouling. If deposits are not excessive, the plug can be cleaned.

OIL FOULED
• Identified by wet black deposits on the insulator shell bore electrodes.
• Caused by excessive oil entering combustion chamber through worn rings and pistons, excessive clearance between valve guides and stems, or worn or loose bearings. Can be cleaned. If engine is not repaired, use a hotter plug.

CARBON FOULED
• Identified by black, dry fluffy carbon deposits on insulator tips, exposed shell surfaces and electrodes.
• Caused by too cold a plug, weak ignition, dirty air cleaner, too rich a fuel mixture, or excessive idling. Can be cleaned.

LEAD FOULED
• Identified by dark gray, black, yellow, or tan deposits or a fused glazed coating on the insulator tip.
• Caused by highly leaded gasoline. Can be cleaned.

WORN
• Identified by severely eroded or worn electrodes.
• Caused by normal wear. Should be replaced.

FUSED SPOT DEPOSIT
• Identified by melted or spotty deposits resembling bubbles or blisters.
• Caused by sudden acceleration. Can be cleaned.

OVERHEATING
• Identified by a white or light gray insulator with small black or gray brown spots and with bluish-burnt appearance of electrodes.
• Caused by engine overheating, wrong type of fuel, loose spark plugs, too hot a plug, or incorrect ignition timing. Replace the plug.

PREIGNITION
• Identified by melted electrodes and possibly blistered insulator. Metallic deposits on insulator indicate engine damage.
• Caused by wrong type of fuel, incorrect ignition timing or advance, too hot a plug, burned valves, or engine overheating. Replace the plug.

Breaker Points

Normal use of a motorcycle causes the breaker points to burn and pit gradually. If they are not pitted too badly, they can be dressed with a few strokes of a clean point file.

CAUTION
Do not use emery cloth or sandpaper to dress the points as particles can remain on the points and cause arcing and burning.

If a few strokes of the file do not smooth the points completely, replace them.

Oil or dirt may get on the points, resulting in poor performance or even premature failure. Common causes for this condition are defective oil seals, improper or excessive breaker cam lubrication, or lack of care when the breaker point cover is removed.

Points should be cleaned and regapped every 1,500-2,000 miles (2,000-3,000 kilometers). To clean the points, first dress them lightly with a clean point file, then remove all residue with lacquer thinner. Close the points on a piece of clean white paper (such as a business card). Continue to pull the card through the closed points until no discoloration or residue remains on the card. Finally, rotate the engine and observe the points as they open and close. If they do not meet squarely, replace them.

To adjust the points, proceed as follows.

1. Remove breaker point cover (**Figure 13**).

2. Remove the alternator cover (**Figure 14**) and turn engine over until one set of points is open to the maximum gap.

3. Measure the breaker point gap with a feeler gauge (**Figure 15**). Point gap should be 0.012-0.016 in. (0.30-0.40mm). If so, go on to Step 7. If adjustment is necessary, continue with Steps 4 through 9.

4. Refer to **Figure 16**. Slightly loosen breaker point retaining screws.

5. Insert a screwdriver into pry slots, then move the stationary contact so that the point gap is 0.014 in. (0.35mm) as shown in **Figure 16**.

6. Tighten both retaining screws, then check gap again. Readjust if necessary.

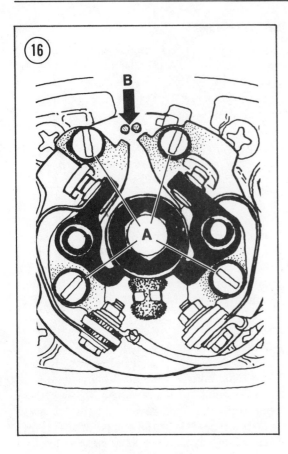

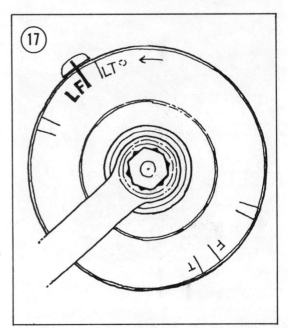

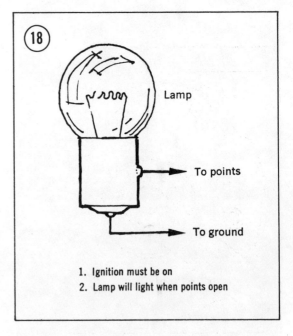

1. Ignition must be on
2. Lamp will light when points open

7. Repeat Steps 2 through 6 on remaining set of points.

8. Wipe the breaker cam clean, then apply a very small quantity of breaker cam lubricant. Apply just enough to create an oil film on the cam; more may cause point failure. This lubricant is sold at any auto parts store.

9. Adjust ignition timing (refer to *Ignition Timing,* following section).

To replace breaker points, disconnect wire which is attached to the movable contact, then remove both retaining screws. Be sure to adjust point gap and ignition timing after installation.

Ignition Timing

Any change in breaker point gap, either from normal wear or from breaker point service, affects ignition timing. If spark plugs fire too early, severe engine damage may result. Overheating and loss of power will occur if the spark occurs too late.

1. Remove the breaker point cover and alternator cover (refer to **Figures 13 and 14**).

2. Place a wrench on the alternator bolt and turn the engine over until the LF mark on the alternator rotor aligns with the index pointer (**Figure 17**).

3. Connect a timing tester to the left-hand breaker point terminal and a good ground (follow the manufacturer's hook-up instructions). If no timing tester is available, make up a test lamp as shown in **Figure 18**.

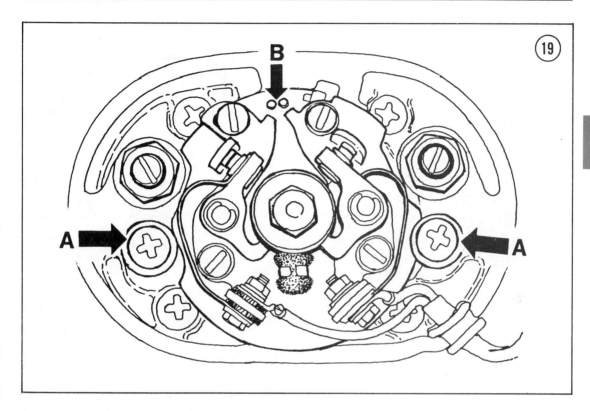

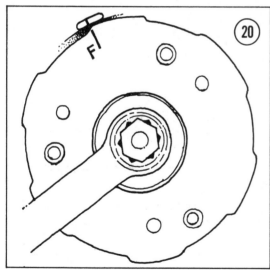

4. Loosen both of the left-hand points base plate retaining screws (A, **Figure 19**) just enough so that the base plate can be moved slightly.

5. Insert a screwdriver in the pry slots (refer to **B, Figure 19**) and rotate the base plate until the left-hand points just begin to open. (If a test lamp is used to determine point opening, be sure that the ignition switch is ON.) The test lamp will light exactly at the moment that the LF mark on the alternator rotor aligns with the index pointer, if the ignition timing is correct.

6. Tighten both base plate retaining screws (refer to A, **Figure 19**).

7. Recheck adjustment by turning rotor clockwise slightly, then counterclockwise slowly. The LF mark and index should align just as the left-hand points open (and the test lamp lights up). Readjust if necessary.

8. Turn rotor counterclockwise until F mark aligns with the index (**Figure 20**).

9. Connect the timing tester to the right-hand points.

10. Slightly loosen both right-hand stationary breaker contact retaining screws, then pry stationary contact slightly one way or the other until the points just begin to open.

> NOTE: *The point gap will change slightly; this is normal.*

11. Tighten both retaining screws.

12. Recheck adjustment by turning rotor clockwise slightly, then counterclockwise slow-

ly. The right-hand points should open just as the F mark and index align. Readjust if necessary.

Air Cleaner Service

During the tune-up, the air cleaner element should be cleaned or replaced.

1. Remove the clamps and retaining nuts and lift the air cleaner off (**Figures 21 and 22**).

2. Remove the element and tap it gently against the palm of your hand to dislodge dirt from the outside. Then blow compressed air gently from the inside. Replace a damaged element, or one that is too dirty to clean satisfactorily.

3. Install by reversing the preceding steps.

Carburetor Adjustment

1. Start engine and allow to warm to operating temperature, then shut it off.

2. Turn each idle mixture screw in until it seats lightly, then back out each one 1¼ turns (**Figure 23**).

3. Start the engine. Adjust each idle speed screw so that the engine idles at 1,000-2,000 rpm (**Figure 24**).

4. Place one hand behind each muffler and adjust idle speed screw (refer to **Figure 24**) until exhaust pressure from each muffler is equal.

5. Turn left cylinder idle mixture screw in either direction, slowly, until engine idle speed is at its maximum.

6. Repeat Step 5 for the right cylinder.

7. Check exhaust pressure from each cylinder (as in Step 4) and adjust either idle speed screw necessary to equalize pressures.

8. Turn each idle speed screw an equal amount to obtain 1,000-1,200 rpm idle speed.

If the preceding procedure does not work well, due to both carburetors being too far out of adjustment, use the following procedure:

1. Turn the idle mixture screw on each carburetor in until it seats lightly, then back the screw out 1¼ turns (refer to **Figure 23**).

2. Start the engine, then ride the bike long enough to warm it thoroughly.

3. Stop the engine and disconnect either spark plug lead (**Figure 25**).

4. Restart the engine on one cylinder. Turn the idle speed screw on the "working" carburetor in enough to keep the engine running (refer to **Figure 24**).

5. Turn the idle speed screw out until the engine runs slower and begins to falter.

6. Turn the idle mixture screw in or out to make the engine run smoothly. Note the speed indicated by the tachometer.

7. Repeat Steps 5 and 6 to achieve the lowest possible stable idle speed.

8. Stop the engine, then reconnect the spark plug lead that was disconnected.

9. Repeat Steps 3 through 8 for the other cylinder, matching the engine speed with that observed in Step 6.

10. Start the engine, then turn each idle speed screw an equal amount until the engine idles at 1,000-1,200 rpm.

11. Place one hand behind each muffler and check that the exhaust pressures are equal (**Figure 26**). If not, turn either idle speed screw in or out until the pressures are equal.

CLUTCH ADJUSTMENT

Adjust the clutch at 1,000 mile (1,500 kilometer) intervals, or whenever necessary.

1. Refer to **Figure 27**. Loosen locknut, then turn cable adjuster until cable is all of the way into the clutch lever bracket.

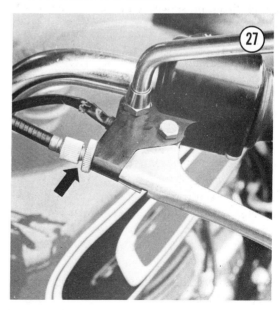

2. Refer to **Figure 28**. Loosen locknut, then turn lower cable adjuster in direction indicated to fully loosen cable.

3. Refer to **Figure 29**. Loosen locknut, then turn adjuster screw counterclockwise until it meets resistance. From this point on, turn it clockwise ¼ turn. Tighten the locknut.

4. Refer to **Figure 28**. Turn lower cable adjuster so that there is approximately ¾ in. (20mm) free play at the clutch hand lever, then tighten lower cable adjuster locknut.

5. Tighten upper cable adjuster locknut. Minor adjustments can then be made at the upper cable adjuster.

BRAKES

Adjust brakes every 1,000 miles (1,500 kilometers), or whenever necessary.

Front (Disc) Brake Adjustment

The front disc brake is self adjusting and needs no periodic maintenance other than brake pad replacement.

Rear (Drum) Brake Adjustment

The rear drum brake is operated by a rod. Simply turn the adjusting nut (**Figure 30**) until the rear brake pedal has approximately ¾-1 in. (20-25mm) of free play (**Figure 31**).

STEERING STEM BEARINGS

Check steering bearings for looseness or binding. *If any exists, find out the cause and correct it immediately.* Refer to Chapter Seven, *Steering Stem* section, for repair procedures.

Adjustment

1. Remove steering stem nut (**Figure 32**).

2. Loosen pinch bolt, then tighten or loosen the ring nut by tapping it gently with a suitable drift until the steering stem turns freely throughout its full travel without excessive looseness or binding (**Figure 33**). Tighten the pinch bolt securely.

3. Tighten the steering stem nut securely (refer to **Figure 32**).

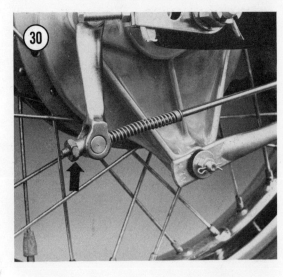

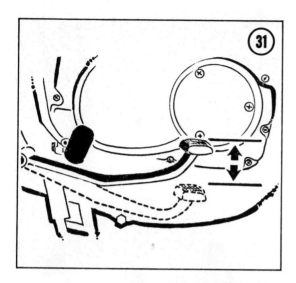

Table **3** TIRE INFLATION

Tire Size	Inflation Pressure (psi)
2.50-18	23
2.75-18	23
3.00-18	23
3.25-18	23
3.50-18	23
4.00-18	23
3.00-19	23
3.25-19	23

WHEELS AND TIRES

Check wheels for bent rims and loose or missing spokes. Complete wheel inspection and service procedures are detailed in Chapter Seven, *Wheels* section.

Check tires for worn treads, cuts, and proper inflation. Refer to **Table 3**.

BATTERY

The battery should always be clean and the cells filled (but not overfilled) with distilled water. Most batteries are marked with electrolyte level limit lines. Always maintain the fluid level between these two lines. (Distilled water is available at most supermarkets).

Overfilling leads to loss of electrolyte, resulting in poor battery performance, short life, and excessive corrosion. Never allow the electrolyte level to fall below the top of the battery plates, as the plates could become permanently damaged due to contact with the air.

Excessive battery water consumption is an indication that the battery is being overcharged. The two most common causes of overcharging are high battery temperature or high voltage regulator setting.

WARNING

When working with batteries, use extreme care to avoid spilling or splashing electrolyte. This electrolyte is sulfuric acid, which can destroy clothing and cause serious chemical burns. Neutralize spilled battery acid immediately with a solution of baking soda and water, then flush away with clean water.

Safety glasses should be worn when working near a battery, to avoid having electrolyte splashed into the eyes. If electrolyte comes into contact with the eyes, force the eyes open and flood with cool clean water for about 5 minutes, and call a physician immediately.

Battery Charging

WARNING

When batteries are being charged, highly explosive gas forms in each cell. Some of this gas escapes through the filler openings and may form an explosive atmosphere around the battery (which may last for several hours). Keep sparks, open flame, or lighted cigarettes away from a battery under charge, or in a room where one has been recently charged. A common cause of battery explosions is the disconnection of a live circuit at a battery terminal (a spark usually occurs under these condition). To avoid this, be sure that the power switch is off before making or breaking connections. (Poor connections are also a common cause of electrical arcs which cause explosions.)

Motorcycle batteries are not designed for high charge or discharge rates. For this reason, it is recommended that a motorcycle battery be charged at a rate not exceeding 10 percent of its ampere-hour capacity.

Example: Do not exceed 0.5 ampere charging rate for a 5 ampere-hour battery, or 1.5 amperes for a 15 ampere-hour battery.

This charge rate should continue for 10 hours if the battery is completely discharged, or until specific gravity of each cell is up to 1.260-1.280, corrected for temperature. If after prolonged charging, specific gravity of one or more cells does not come up to at least 1.230, the battery will not perform as well as it should, but it may continue to provide satisfactory service for a time.

Some temperature rise is normal as a battery is being charged. Do not allow electrolyte temperature to exceed 110 degrees F. Should temperature reach that figure, discontinue charging until the battery cools, then resume charging at a lower rate.

Testing State of Charge

Place the tube of a hydrometer into the filler opening and draw in just enough electrolyte to lift the float (**Figure 34**). Hold the instrument in a vertical position and read specific gravity on the scale, where the float stem emerges from the electrolyte.

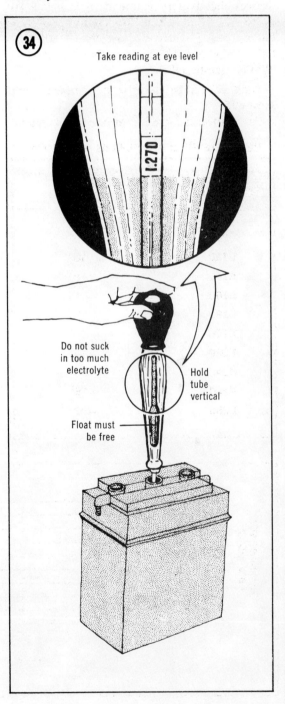

Specific gravity of the electrolyte varies with temperature, so it is necessary to apply a temperature correction to the reading so obtained. For each 10 degrees that battery temperature exceeds 80 degrees F, add 0.004 to the indicated specific gravity. Likewise, subtract 0.004 from the indicated value for each 10 degrees that battery temperature is below 80 degrees F. Repeat this measurement for each battery cell. If there is more than 0.050 differences (50 points) between cells, battery condition is questionable.

State of charge may be determined from **Figure 35**.

Don't measure specific gravity immediately

after adding water. Ride the machine a few miles to ensure mixture of the electrolyte.

It is most important to maintain batteries fully charged during cold weather. A fully charged battery freezes at a much lower temperature than one which is partially discharged. Freezing temperature depends on specific gravity. Refer to **Table 4**.

Battery Cables

Keep battery cables tight and clean (free of corrosion, grease, etc.). If the cables are corroded, disconnect them and clean them separately with a wire brush and a baking soda and water solution. After cleaning, apply a thin coating of petroleum jelly to the battery terminals before installing the cables. After connecting the cables, apply a light coating to the connection. This procedure will help to prevent future corrosion.

DRIVE CHAIN

Clean, lubricate, and adjust the drive chain every 1,000 miles (1,500 kilometers), or whenever necessary. The drive chain becomes worn after prolonged use. Wear in pins, bushings, and rollers causes chain stretch. Sliding action between roller surfaces and sprocket teeth also contribute to wear.

Cleaning and Adjustment

1. Disconnect the master link (**Figure 36**) and remove chain.

Table 4 SPECIFIC GRAVITY/FREEZING TEMPERATURE

Specific Gravity	Freezing Temperature Degrees F
1.100	18
1.120	13
1.140	8
1.160	1
1.180	−6
1.200	−17
1.220	−31
1.240	−50
1.260	−75
1.280	−92

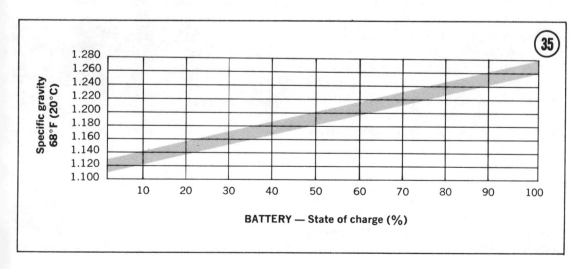

2. Clean chain thoroughly with solvent.

3. Rinse chain with clean solvent, then blow dry with compressed air.

4. Examine chain carefully for wear or damage. Replace if there is any doubt as to its condition. If chain is OK, lubricate by soaking in oil, or any of the special chain lubricants available in any motorcycle shop.

5. Install the chain. Be sure master link is installed as shown in **Figure 36**.

6. Refer to **Figure 37**. Proceed with chain adjustment, as follows:

   a. Remove cotter pin and loosen rear axle nut.

   b. Loosen locknut on each side.

   c. There is one adjustment bolt on each side. Turn it until there is ¾-1 in. (20-25mm) of up and down movement in the center of the lower chain run (**Figure 38**).

   d. Be sure that the reference marks on the swinging arm and the index mark on the chain adjuster (refer to **Figure 37**) are in the same relative positions on each side.

7. Tighten the rear axle nut then install a new cotter pin (refer to **Figure 37**).

8. Adjust the rear brake (refer to *Brakes* section, this chapter).

FORK OIL

Replacement

Replace the fork oil every 3,000 miles (4,500 kilometers), as follows:

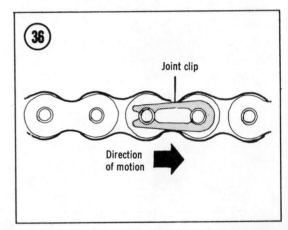

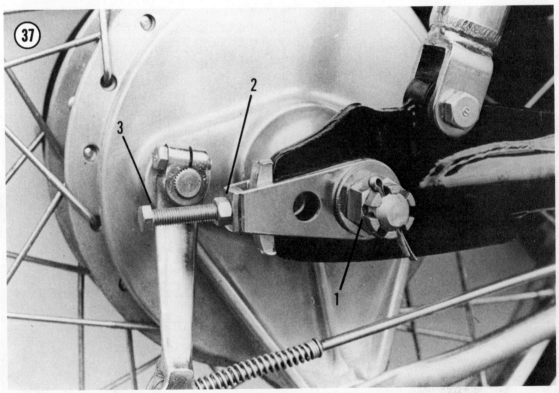

1. Rear axle nut   2. Locknut   3. Adjustment bolt

1. Place a pan under each fork leg, then remove drain plug at lower end of each fork leg (**Figure 39**). Allow oil to drain out into pan.

> NOTE: *To aid in removing all of the oil, push down on the forks several times to force oil out.*

2. Install the drain plugs, then remove upper fork bolts (**Figure 40**) and pour fresh fork oil into forks. Capacity is 5.4-5.6 oz. (160-165cc) for all models.

3. Install upper fork bolts.

OIL AND OIL FILTER

Probably the single most important maintenance item which contributes to long engine life is that of regular oil changes. Engine oil becomes contaminated with products of combustion, condensation, and dirt. Some of these contaminants react with oil, forming acids which attack vital engine components, and thereby result in premature wear.

To change engine oil, ride the bike until it is thoroughly warm, then place a pan under the engine and remove the engine oil drain plug (**Figure 41**). Allow the oil to drain thoroughly (it may help to rock the motorcycle from side to side, and also forward and backward, to get as much oil out as possible).

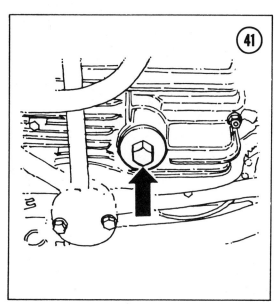

Install the engine oil drain plug and refill with fresh engine oil. Refer to **Table 5** for recommended grades. Capacity is 3.2 U.S. pints (1.5 liters).

Be sure to check for leaks after the oil change is complete.

Maintain the engine oil level between both level marks on the dipstick (**Figure 42**).

> NOTE: *The dipstick should not be screwed into the engine when checking oil level.*

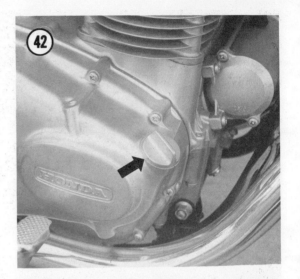

All models are equipped with a centrifugal oil filter which separates sludge and other foreign particles from the engine oil before it is distributed throughout the engine. To clean the filter, proceed as follows:

1. Remove oil filter cover (**Figure 43**).

2. Remove internal circlip holding oil filter cap (**Figure 44**).

3. Remove oil filter cap (**Figure 45**).

4. Clean cap in solvent and install with a new O-ring. Secure with internal circlip (refer to **Figure 44**).

5. Install oil filter cover with a new gasket (refer to **Figure 43**). Use a sealer such as Gasgacinch.

SWINGING ARM

Disassemble the swinging arm and grease its pivot shaft and bushings every 6,000 miles (9,000 kilometers). Refer to **Figure 46** for the following steps:

1. Remove hex nut, washer, and dust seal cap.

2. Slide the pivot bolt out of the center collar.

3. Remove center collar. Grease inside of the pivot bushing; inside and outside of center collar; and outside of pivot bolt.

4. Assemble by reversing the preceding steps.

Table 5   OIL GRADES

Temperature Range	Oil Grade
Below 32 degrees F	10W
32 to 60 degrees F	20W
Above 60 degrees F	30W

2

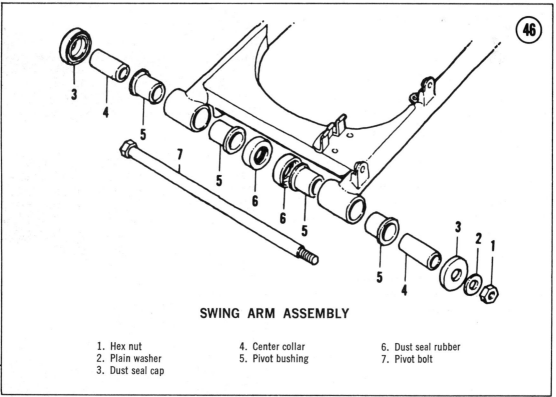

SWING ARM ASSEMBLY

1. Hex nut
2. Plain washer
3. Dust seal cap

4. Center collar
5. Pivot bushing

6. Dust seal rubber
7. Pivot bolt

CHAPTER THREE

TROUBLESHOOTING

Diagnosing motorcycle ills is relatively simple if you use orderly procedures and keep a few basic principles in mind.

Never assume anything. Don't overlook the obvious. If you are riding along and the bike suddenly quits, check the easiest, most accesible problem spots first. Is there gasoline in the tank? Is the gas petcock in the ON or RESERVE position? Has a spark plug wire fallen off? Check the ignition switch. Sometimes the weight of keys on a key ring may turn the ignition off suddenly.

If nothing obvious turns up in a cursory check, look a little further. Learning to recognize and describe symptoms will make repairs easier for you or a mechanic at the shop. Describe problems accurately and fully. Saying that "it won't run" isn't the same as saying "it quit on the highway at high speed and wouldn't start," or that "it sat in my garage for three months and then wouldn't start."

Gather as many symptoms together as possible to aid in diagnosis. Note whether the engine lost power gradually or all at once, what color smoke (if any) came from the exhausts, and so on. Remember that the more complicated a machine is, the easier it is to troubleshoot because symptoms point to specific problems.

You don't need fancy equipment or complicated test gear to determine whether repairs can be attempted at home. A few simple checks could save a large repair bill and time lost while the bike sits in a dealer's service department. On the other hand, be realistic and don't attempt repairs beyond your abilities. Service departments tend to charge heavily for putting together a disassembled engine that may have been abused. Some places won't even take on such a job — so use common sense and don't get in over your head.

OPERATING REQUIREMENTS

An engine needs three basics to run properly: correct gas-air mixture, compression, and a spark at the right time. If one or more are missing the engine won't run. The electrical system is the weakest link of the three. More problems result from electrical breakdowns than from any other source. Keep that in mind before you begin tampering with carburetor adjustments and the like.

If a bike has been sitting for any length of time and refuses to start, check the battery for a charged condition first and then look to the gasoline delivery system. This includes the tank, fuel petcocks, lines and the carburetor. Rust may have formed in the tank, obstructing fuel flow. Gasoline deposits may have gummed up carburetor jets and air passages. Gasoline tends to lose its potency after standing for long periods. Condensation may contaminate it with water. Drain old gas and try starting with a fresh tankful. Drain carburetor bowls too.

Compression, or the lack of it, usually enters the picture only in the case of older machines. Worn or broken pistons, rings, and cylinder bores could prevent starting. Generally, a gradual power loss and harder and harder starting will be readily apparent in this case.

STARTING DIFFICULTIES

Check gas flow first. Remove the gas cap and look into the tank. If gas is present, pull off a fuel line at the carburetor and see if gas flows freely. If none comes out, the fuel tap may be shut off, blocked by rust or foreign matter, or the fuel line may be stopped up or kinked. If the carburetor is getting usable fuel, turn to the electrical system next.

Check that the battery is charged by turning on the lights or by blowing the horn. Refer to your owner's manual for starting procedures with a dead battery. Have the battery recharged if necessary.

Pull off a spark plug cap, remove the spark plug and reconnect the cap. Lay the plug against the cylinder head so its base makes a good connection and turn the engine over with the kickstarter. A fat, blue spark should jump across the electrodes. If there is no spark, or a weak one, there is electrical system trouble. Check for a defective plug by replacing it with a known good one. Don't assume that a plug is good just because it's new.

Once the plug has been cleared of guilt, but there's still no spark, start backtracking through the system. If the contact at the end of the spark plug wire can be exposed it can be held about ⅛ inch from the head while the engine is turned over to check for a spark. Remember to hold the wire only by its insulation to avoid a nasty shock. If the plug wires are dirty, greasy, or wet, wrap a rag around them so you won't get shocked. If you do feel a shock or see sparks along the wire, clean or replace the wire and/or its connections.

If there's no spark at the plug wire, look for loose connections at the coil and battery. If all seems in order there, check next for oily or dirty contact points. Clean points with electrical contact cleaner or a strip of paper. On battery ignition models, with the ignition switch turned on, open and close the points manually with a screwdriver.

No spark at the points with this test indicates a failure in the ignition system. Refer to *Ignition System Problems,* this chapter, for checkout procedures.

Refer to Chapter Two, *Ignition Timing* section for checking and setting ignition timing.

Note that spark plugs of the incorrect heat range (too cold) may cause hard starting. Set gaps to specifications. If you have just ridden through a puddle or washed the bike and it won't start, dry off plugs and plug wires. Water may have entered the carburetor and fouled the fuel under these conditions, but wet plugs and wires are the more likely problem.

If a healthy spark occurs at the right time, and there is adequate gas flow to the carburetor, check the carburetor itself at this time. Make sure all jets and air passages are clean, check float level and adjust if necessary. Shake the float to check for gasoline inside it and replace or repair as indicated. Check that the carburetors are mounted snugly and no air is leaking past the manifolds. Check for a clogged air filter.

Compression may be checked in the field by turning the kickstarter by hand and noting that adequate resistance is felt, or by removing a spark plug and placing a finger over the plug hole and feeling for pressure. Refer to Chapter Two for details on performing an engine compression test.

POOR IDLING

Poor idling may be caused by incorrect carburetor adjustment, incorrect timing, or ignition system defects. Check the gas cap vent for an obstruction.

MISFIRING

Misfirings can be caused by a weak spark or dirty plugs. Check for fuel contamination. Run the machine at night or in a darkened garage to check for spark leaks along the plug wires and under the spark plug cap. If misfiring occurs only at certain throttle settings, refer to the carburetor chapter for the specific carburetor circuits involved. Misfiring under heavy load, as when climbing hills or accelerating, is usually caused by bad spark plugs.

FLAT SPOTS

Poor condition of rings, pistons, or cylinders will cause a lack of power and speed. Ignition timing should be checked.

OVERHEATING

If the engine seems to run too hot all the time, be sure you are not idling it for long periods. Air cooled engines are not designed to operate at a standstill for any length of time. Heavy stop and go traffic is hard on a motorcycle engine. Spark plugs of the wrong heat range can burn pistons. An excessively lean gas mixture may cause overheating. Check ignition timing. Don't ride in too high a gear. Broken or worn rings and valves may permit compression gases to leak past them, heating heads and cylinders excessively. Check oil level and use the proper grade lubricants.

BACKFIRING

Check that timing is not advanced too far. Check fuel for contamination.

ENGINE NOISES

Experience is needed to diagnose accurately in this area. Noises are hard to differentiate and harder yet to describe. Deep knocking noises usually mean main bearing failure. A slapping noise generally comes from loose pistons. A light knocking noise during acceleration may be a bad connecting rod bearing. Pinging, which sounds like marbles being shaken in a tin can, is caused by ignition advanced too far or gasoline with too low an octane rating. Pinging should be corrected immediately or damage to pistons will result. Compression leaks at the head-cylinder joint will sound like a rapid on and off squeal.

PISTON SEIZURE

Piston seizure is caused by incorrect piston clearances when fitted, fitting rings with improper end gap, too thin an oil being used, incorrect spark plug heat range, or incorrect ignition timing. Overheating from any cause may result in seizure.

EXCESSIVE VIBRATION

Excessive vibration may be caused by loose motor mounts, worn engine or transmission bearings, loose wheels, worn swinging arm bushings, a generally poor running engine, broken or cracked frame, or one that has been damaged in a collision. See also *Poor Handling*.

CLUTCH SLIP OR DRAG

Clutch slip may be due to worn plates, improper adjustment, or glazed plates. A dragging clutch could result from damaged or bent plates, improper adjustment, or even clutch spring pressure.

POOR HANDLING

Poor handling may be caused by improper tire pressures, a damaged frame or swinging arm, worn shocks or front forks, weak fork springs, a bent or broken steering stem, misaligned wheels, loose or missing spokes, worn tires, bent handlebars, worn wheel bearings or dragging brakes.

BRAKE PROBLEMS

Sticking brakes may be caused by broken or weak return springs, improper cable or rod adjustment, or dry pivot and cam bushings. Grabbing brakes may be caused by greasy linings which must be replaced. Brake grab may also be due to out-of-round drums or linings which have broken loose from the brake shoes. Glazed linings or glazed brake pads will cause loss of stopping power.

IGNITION SYSTEM PROBLEMS

Honda twin-cylinder models are equipped with a battery and coil ignition system, similiar

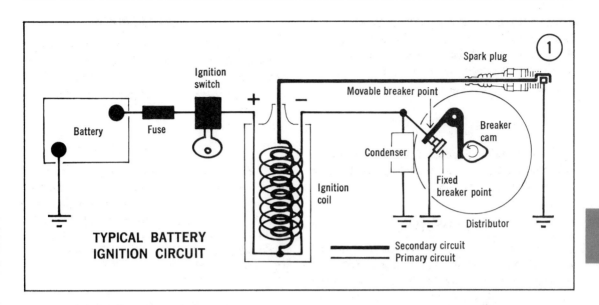

TYPICAL BATTERY
IGNITION CIRCUIT

Table 1   IGNITION SYSTEM PROBLEMS

Symptom	Probable Cause	Remedy
No spark or weak spark	Discharged battery	Charge battery
	Defective fuse	Replace
	Defective main switch	Replace
	Loose or corroded connections	Clean and tighten
	Broken wire	Repair
	Incorrect point gap	Reset points. Be sure to readjust ignition timing
	Dirty or oily points	Clean points
	Spark plug lead damaged	Replace wire
	Broken primary wire	Repair wire
	Open winding in coil	Replace coil
	Shorted winding in coil	Replace coil
	Defective condenser	Replace condenser

in many ways to that of a conventional automobile.

Figure 1 illustrates a typical battery ignition system for a single cylinder. Refer to that illustration during the following discussion.

Ignition system problems can be classified as no spark, weak spark, or improperly timed spark. **Table 1** lists common causes and remedies for ignition system malfunctions.

Disconnect the condenser and the wire from the points. Connect the ungrounded (positive) voltmeter lead to the wire which was connected to the points. If the voltmeter does not indicate battery voltage, the problem is an open coil primary circuit. Replace the suspected coil with a known good one. If the coil doesn't work, the problem is in the primary winding.

If the voltmeter indicates battery voltage, the coil primary circuit is OK. Connect the positive voltmeter lead to the wire which goes from the coil to the points. Block the points open with a business card or similar piece of cardboard. Connect the negative voltmeter lead to the movable point. If the voltmeter indicates any voltage, the points are shorted and must be replace.

If the foregoing checks are satisfactory, the problem is in the coil or condenser. Substitute each of these separately with a known good one to determine which is defective.

Ignition Coil

The ignition coil (**Figure 2**) is a form of transformer which develops the high voltage required to jump the spark plug gap. The only maintenance required is that of keeping the electrical connections clean and tight, and occasionally checking to see that the coil is mounted securely.

If the condition of the coil is doubtful, there are several checks which should be made.

1. Measure resistance between both primary terminals of the suspected coil. Resistance should be approximately 3 to 5 ohms.

2. Measure secondary coil resistance between either primary lead and the secondary lead of the suspected coil. Resistance should be approximately 10,000 ohms.

3. Set the meter on the highest ohmmeter range. Determine that there is no continuity between the high voltage lead and coil frame.

Condenser

The condenser is a sealed unit that requires no maintenance. Be sure that both connections are clean and tight.

Two tests can be made on the condenser. Measure condenser capacity with a condenser tester. Capacity should be about 0.2-0.3 microfarad. The other test is insulation resistance, which should not be less than 5 megohms, measured between the condenser pigtail and case.

In the event that no test equipment is available, a quick test of the condenser may be made by connecting the condenser case to the negative terminal of the motorcycle battery, and the positive lead to the positive battery terminal. Allow the condenser to charge for a few seconds, then quickly disconnect the battery and touch the condenser pigtail to the condenser case. If you observe a spark as the pigtail touches the case, you may assume that the condenser is OK.

Arching between the breaker points is a common symptom of condenser failure.

CHARGING SYSTEM

The charging system (**Figure 3**) on all Honda twins covered by this manual consists of an alternator, battery, and interconnecting wiring. Some models are also equipped with a solid state voltage regulator.

Alternator

An alternator (**Figure 4**) is a form of electrical generator in which a magnetized field rotor revolves within a set of stationary coils called a stator. As the rotor revolves, alternating current is induced in the stator. Stator current is then rectified and used to operate electrical accessories on the motorcycle and for battery charging.

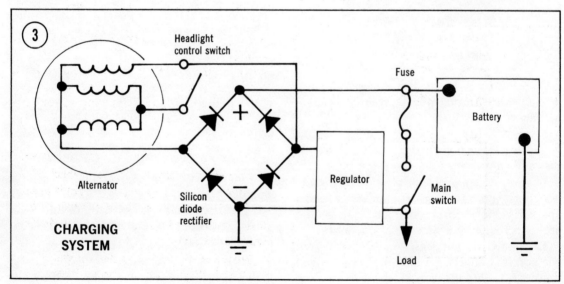

Table 2   ALTERNATOR OUTPUT

Model	Charging Starts	Test Rpm	Minimum Voltage	Current (Amperes)
250	2,000	5,000	14.8	1.2 maximum
		10,000	15.5	4.0 maximum
360	2,100	5,000	14.8	1.2 minimum
		10,000	15.5	4.0 maximum

Table 3   TEST POINTS/RESISTANCE

Test Points	Resistance
Yellow - pink	1.1 ohm
Yellow/white - pink or white	0.5 ohm

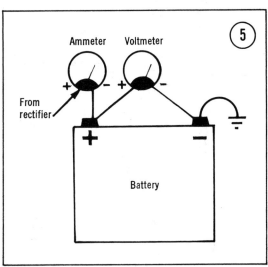

If alternator or regulator problems are suspected, as in the case of a chronically undercharged battery or dim headlights, first check the battery (refer to *Battery Service*). It must be in good condition and at least half charged (1.220 specific gravity) before meaningful interpretation of test results can be made.

Connect 0-15 DC voltmeter and 0-10 DC ammeter as shown in **Figure 5**. Connect the positive ammeter terminal to the battery charging wire from the rectifier, and the negative ammeter terminal to the positive battery terminal. Connect the voltmeter positive lead to the battery charging lead and the negative terminal to a good ground.

CAUTION
If the ammeter is connected between the battery positive terminal and the starter cable, do not attempt to start the engine with the electric starter. Starter current will burn out the ammeter.

Start the engine and run it at the speeds listed in **Table 2**. Observe the voltmeter and ammeter and compare their indications with the specification. All measurements are made with lights on.

If charging current was considerably lower than specified, check the alternator and rectifier. Less likely is that charging current was too high; in that case, the regulator is probably at fault.

To check the alternator, proceed as follows.

1. Remove the alternator stator, then check for continuity between each pair of leads coming from it. If resistance between any pair of leads differs greatly from that specified in **Table 3**, replace the stator.

2. Set the ohmmeter to its highest range, then check that there is no continuity between any

lead and the stator frame. Replace the stator if there is any shorted lead.

3. Check all coils and wiring for chafing, broken connections, etc. Repair or replace as required.

4. Alternator rotors occasionally lose magnetism as a result of old age, presence of strong magnetic fields, or a sharp blow. Should the situation occur, it must be replaced.

Rectifier

All models are equipped with full-wave bridge rectifiers (refer to **Figure 6**). Checking procedures are similar for all; but the rectifiers differ in lead colors and connectors.

Some rectifiers mount by one terminal. The other terminals are leads, colored yellow, brown, and red/white. To test this rectifier, disconnect it from the motorcycle, then using an ohmmeter, measure resistance in both directions between the following pairs of terminals.

a. Yellow and ground
b. Brown and ground
c. Yellow and red/white
d. Brown and red/white

The second type rectifier has 4 leads, colored green, yellow, red/white or brown/white, and pink. To test this rectifier, measure resistance between each pair of wires listed:

a. Green and yellow
b. Green and pink
c. Yellow and red/white or brown/white
d. Pink and red/white or brown/white

On any type rectifier, resistance between each pair should be very high in one direction and low in the other. If resistance is either very high or very low in either direction, replace the rectifier assembly.

Always handle the rectifier assembly carefully. Do not bend or try to rotate the wafers. Do not loosen the screw which holds the assembly together. Moisture can damage the assembly, so keep it dry.

Never run the engine with the battery disconnected or without a fuse; doing so can cause immediate rectifier destruction.

Voltage Regulator

Problems with the voltage regulator (**Figure 7**) are rare. The simplest way to test it is to connect the test circuit shown in **Figure 5**, and

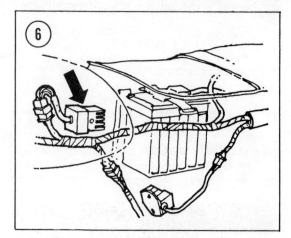

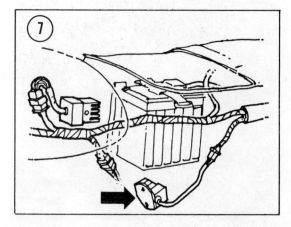

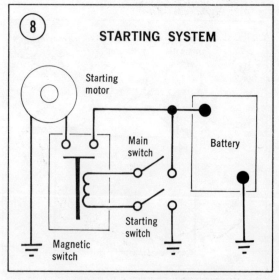

STARTING SYSTEM

Starting motor

Main switch

Battery

Starting switch

Magnetic switch

compare battery charging current at various engine speeds with the regulator connected and disconnected. If charging current is limited to those values specified in **Table 2** when the regulator is connected, it is in good condition.

CAUTION
Do not disconnect or connect the regulator with the engine running.

ELECTRIC STARTER PROBLEMS

Figure 8 is a diagram of a typical starting system, showing the location of each component.

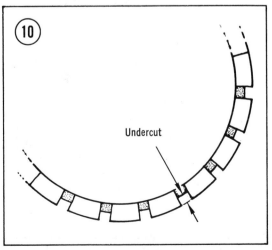

Undercut

Circuit Operation

When the rider presses starter pushbutton, current flows from battery through the coil of starter relay if main switch is closed. Current through the relay coil causes its plunger to be pulled upward, thereby bridging the 2 heavy contacts in the starter relay, and completing the circuit from the battery to the starter motor.

Starter Motor

The starter motor (**Figure 9**) is wound in series for high torque, and draws approximately 120 amperes under normal starting conditions. This figure can vary considerably, depending on engine temperature, starter condition, and other factors.

If starter problems are encountered, overhaul is best performed by a shop specializing in small motor repair or auto electrical systems. Some checks and service can be done by the layman, however.

1. Remove and disassemble the starter motor.

2. If either brush is excessively worn, replace both brushes.

3. Examine the commutator for roughness or burning. Minor roughness may be smoothed with fine sandpaper. After smoothing, be sure that the mica insulators between commutator segments are undercut to a depth of at least 0.012 inch (0.3 millimeter), as shown in **Figure 10**.

4. Use an armature growler or ohmmeter to determine that no commutator segment is shorted to the shaft.

5. Using an ohmmeter, determine that there is continuity between every adjacent pair of commutator segments.

6. With the starter disassembled, determine that there is continuity between the ungrounded brush holder and the starter terminal.

7. Using the highest ohmmeter range, determine that there is no continuity between the starter terminal and starter motor housing.

Table 4 lists symptoms, probable causes, and remedies for possible starter malfunctions.

Starter Drive

The starter turns the engine through a chain and overrunning clutch (**Figure 11**).

3

Table 4   STARTER TROUBLESHOOTING

Symptom	Probable Cause	Remedy
Starter does not work	Low battery	Recharge battery
	Worn brushes	Replace brushes
	Internal short	Repair or replace defective component
	Defective wiring or connections	Repair wire or clean and tighten connections
	Defective switch	Replace switch
Starter action is weak	Low battery	Recharge battery
	Pitted relay contacts	Clean contacts or replace voltage regulator
	Brushes worn	Replace brushes
	Defective wiring or connections	Repair wire or clean and tighten
	Short in armature	Replace armature
Starter runs continuously	Stuck relay	Dress contacts
Starter turns but engine does not	Defective starter drive	Repair or replace starter drive

To check the starter drive, it is only necessary to check that it transmits torque in one direction only. Disassemble the unit and check all springs and rollers in the event of malfunction.

Starter Relay

After long service, contacts in the starter relay may pit and burn, or the coil may burn out. To test this unit, connect the motorycycle battery between the relay coil terminals (usually yellow/red and black). If no click occurs, replace the relay. If the relay clicks, the relay coil is OK, but its contacts may be pitted or burned. To correct this problem, disassemble the starter relay and lightly dress its contacts with a fine file. Don't remove any more metal than necessary.

LIGHTING PROBLEMS

The headlight assembly consists primarily of a headlight lens and reflector unit, and related hardware.

In the event of lighting troubles, first check the affected bulb. Poor ground connections are another cause of lamp malfunctions.

Turn signals usually operate from direct current supplied by the battery. When replacing the signal bulbs, always be sure to use the proper type. Erratic operation or even failure to flash may result from use of wrong bulbs.

Stoplights usually operate from direct current also. Stoplight switches should be adjusted so that the lamp comes on just before braking action begins. Front brake stoplight switches are frequently built into the front brake cable, and are not adjustable.

Bulbs which continuously burn out may be caused by excessive vibration, loose connections that permit sudden current surges, poor battery connections, or installation of the wrong type bulb.

A dead battery, or one which discharges quickly, may be caused by a faulty generator or rectifier. Check for loose or corroded terminals.

Shorted battery cells or broken terminals will keep a battery from charging. Low water level will decrease a battery's capacity. A battery left uncharged after installation will sulphate, rendering it useless. Refer to Chapter Two, *Battery Service* section.

A majority of light and horn or other electrical accessory problems are caused by loose or corroded ground connections. Check those first

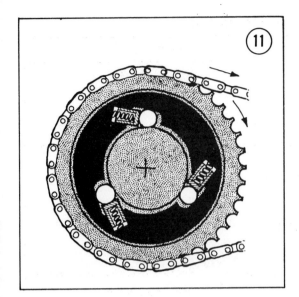

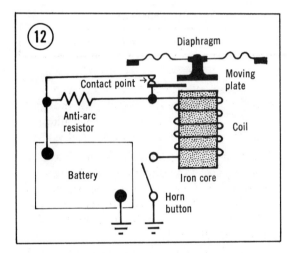

and then substitute known good units for easier troubleshooting.

HORN PROBLEMS

A typical horn circuit is shown in **Figure 12**. Current for the horn is supplied by the battery. One terminal is connected to the battery through the main switch. The other terminal is grounded when the horn button is pressed.

The horn (**Figure 13**) will not sound if its contact points are burned. Dress them with a small point file of flex stone. Adjust horn tone after dressing the contact points (refer to Chapter Six, *Horn* section).

CHAPTER FOUR

ENGINE, TRANSMISSION, AND CLUTCH

This chapter describes removal, disassembly, service, reassembly and installation of the engine, transmission, and clutch. Engine removal is not necessary for service operations on alternators, oil pumps, clutches, or shifter mechanism.

SERVICE HINTS

Experience has shown that work goes faster and easier if certain standard shop practices are observed. Some of the more important ones are listed below.

1. During engine disassembly, keep all related parts together. Reassembly will be much easier if this precaution is taken, in particular if a long period lapses between disassembly and reassembly.

2. All O-rings, gaskets, snap rings, and cotter pins which are removed should be replace.

3. Be sure all parts are clean upon reassembly.

4. Lubricate all moving parts liberally before reassembly.

5. On parts attached with multiple bolts or screws, tighten those of larger diameter first. If parts are attached with inner and outer bolts or screws, tighten inner ones first.

4

PRELIMINARY
ENGINE DISASSEMBLY

It is quite often easier to dismantle the engine as far as possible while it is still mounted in the frame. Proceed as follows:

1. Loosen air filter clamp screw (**Figure 1**), then remove 2 bolts holding air filter in place and remove air filter (**Figures 2 and 3**).

2. Disconnect the push-pull throttle cables from the twist grip and loosen all routing clamps. Remove the carburetor retaining nuts (**Figures 4**) and remove the carburetors from the cylinder head.

3. Remove the footrests (**Figure 5**).

4. Remove the kickstarter (**Figure 6**).

5. Remove bolts in case (**Figure 7**).

6. Slacken brake adjusting nut (**Figure 8**).

7. Tap case with a rubber or plastic mallet to loosen it, then lift case off (**Figure 9**).

> NOTE: *Be sure thrust washer remains on shaft (it can be found inside the case, if it is missing).*

8. On opposite side of engine, remove cover (**Figure 10**).

9. Disconnect clutch cable (**Figure 11**).

10. Remove alternator cover (**Figure 12**).

11. Disconnect electrical plug (**Figure 13**).

12. Disconnect neutral light switch wire (**Figure 14**).

13. Remove alternator housing (3 long and 5 short bolts), then tap cover with a rubber or plastic mallet to loosen it, and remove it (**Figure 15**).

14. Disconnect starter cable (**Figure 16**).

15. Remove starter bolts (**Figure 17**), then remove starter, sprocket, and chain (**Figure 18**).

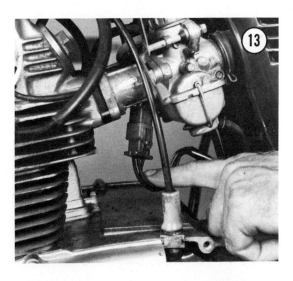

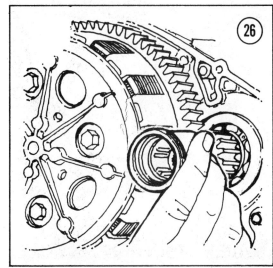

16. Remove sprocket bolts and sprocket (**Figures 19 and 20**).

17. Remove starter cable retaining clips (**Figure 21**).

18. Disconnect the breaker point wire.

19. Remove spark plug wires.

20. Unhook wiring harness from frame clips.

21. Remove screw holding tachometer cable and pull cable out of housing (**Figure 22**).

22. Check engine for any electrical connections, etc., that you may have missed, and disconnect them.

CLUTCH AND OIL PUMP

On all models, the clutch is located under the right crankcase cover, and may be serviced without engine removal.

The oil pump is driven by an eccentric cam on the engine side of the clutch housing which drives a pushrod to operate the oil pump plunger.

Removal

1. Remove snap ring holding the oil filter cap in place, then remove the oil filter cap (**Figures 23 and 24**).

2. Bend the locking tab back, then remove the nut with a special Honda tool (about $4.00 at your Honda dealer). Remove the slotted nut, lockwasher, and dished washer (it is marked OUTSIDE for reassembly purposes). Refer to **Figure 25**.

3. Remove the oil filter housing (**Figure 26**).

4. Remove the oil pump drive gear (**Figure 27**).

5. Remove hex bolts that hold clutch springs (**Figure 28**), and remove the clutch springs. See **Figure 29**).

> NOTE: *Loosen each hex nut a little bit at a time to equalize pressure.*

6. Remove clutch pressure plate and all friction and steel plates as a unit (**Figure 30**).

7. Remove the push crown, then the clutch hub snap ring (**Figure 31**).

8. Remove the clutch hub (**Figure 32**).

9. Remove the clutch housing (**Figure 33**).

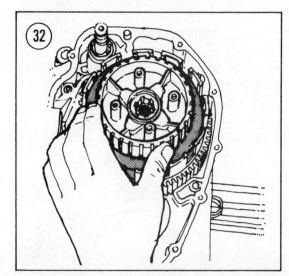

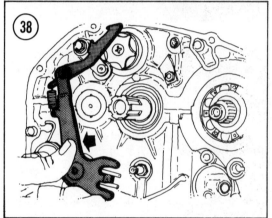

Table 1   CLUTCH DISC SPECIFICATIONS

Model	Standard Thickness	Wear limit
250 and 360	0.106 in. (2.7mm)	0.905 in. (2.3mm)

10. Remove primary drive gear (**Figure 34**).

11. Remove thrust washer, snap ring, and kickstarter return spring (**Figure 35**).

12. Remove shift cam stopper plate (**Figure 36**).

13. On opposite side of engine, remove shift lever, then depress the shift arm from the shift drum (**Figure 37**).

14. Pull out the shift spindle (**Figure 38**).

Inspection

1. Measure thickness of each friction disc with vernier calipers. Replace all discs if any disc is worn to its wear limit, specified in **Table 1**.

2. Place each clutch plate on a flat surface. Using a feeler gauge, measure clutch plate warpage. Replace plates if any plate is warped more than 0.012 in. (0.3mm).

3. Measure free length of each clutch spring. Replace all springs as a set if any spring is shorter than its service limit, specified in **Table 2**.

Installation

Refer to *Clutch and Oil Pump Installation* procedure, later in this chapter.

ENGINE REMOVAL

Engine removal is similar for all models listed in this manual.

1. Warm the engine if possible, then drain engine oil into a pan.

2. Turn fuel petcock selector lever to STOP, then remove fuel lines from fuel petcock.

3. Remove battery cable.

4. Remove gas tank.

5. Perform all steps listed under *Preliminary Engine Dismantling*, earlier in this chapter.

Table 2   CLUTCH SPRING SPECIFICATIONS

Model	Standard Length		Service Limits	
	Inches	Millimeters	Inches	Millimeters
250	1.40	35.5	1.35	34.2
360	1.23	35.5	1.17	29.7

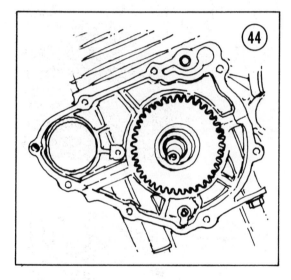

6. Remove top rear engine mounting bolts (**Figure 39**).

7. Remove lower rear engine mounting bolts (**Figure 40**).

8. Remove front lower engine mounting bolts (**Figure 41**).

9. Lift engine out of frame.

10. Remove alternator retaining bolt, then pull the alternator with a puller (**Figures 42 and 43**).

11. Remove the starter sprocket retaining bolt (refer to **Figure 43**), then pull the starter sprocket off (**Figure 44**).

CYLINDER HEAD

Removal

1. Remove the side cover retaining bolts and remove the side covers (one at each end of the cam base).

> NOTE: *It may be necessary to tap the covers loose with a rubber or plastic mallet.*

2. Remove breaker point cover. Remove the 2 screws holding the breaker plate assembly in place (**Figure 45**).

3. Remove the spark advance mechanism center bolt (**Figure 46**), then remove the spark advance mechanism (**Figure 47**).

4. Remove all tappet covers (**Figure 48**).

5. Remove engine breather cover and gasket (**Figure 49**).

6. Remove eight 8mm and six 6mm bolts, then remove cylinder head cover (**Figure 50**).

> NOTE: *Tap the cover with a rubber or plastic mallet to loosen it.*

7. Remove the front cam chain tensioner (**Figure 51**).

8. Remove the retaining bolts, then lift the cam chain tensioner out (**Figure 52**).

9. Remove the camshaft sprocket retaining bolts (**Figure 53**).

> NOTE: *It will be necessary to rotate the crankshaft in order to get at the remaining bolt after removing the first one.*

10. Slip the chain off of the sprocket as shown in **Figure 54**.

11. Slide the camshaft out to the right. Tie a piece of wire to the cam chain and wrap one end of the wire around a stud to keep the chain from dropping down into the engine (**Figure 55**).

> CAUTION
> *When removing the camshaft (refer to Step 11, preceding), do not lose the thrust washer on the left end of the camshaft.*

12. Remove 2 cylinder head retaining bolts (one on each side) as shown in **Figure 56**.

4

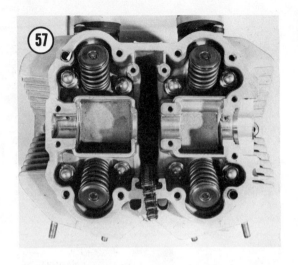

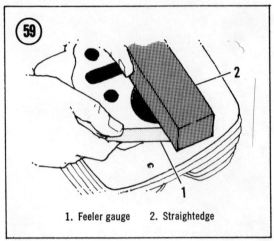

1. Feeler gauge   2. Straightedge

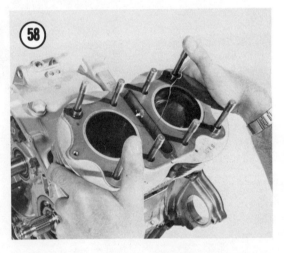

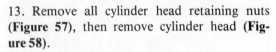

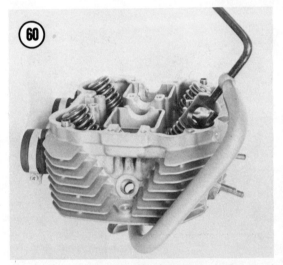

13. Remove all cylinder head retaining nuts (**Figure 57**), then remove cylinder head (**Figure 58**).

Inspection

1. Refer to **Figure 59**. Measure the cylinder head warpage with a straightedge and feeler gauge. Warpage must not exceed 0.002 in. (0.05mm). If clearance exceeds that value, resurface or replace the cylinder head.

2. Remove carbon from each combustion chamber with a wire brush chucked into an electric drill. (This operation is easier with valves still installed in the cylinder head.)

Valve Service

Valve service is best left to a machine shop which has the experience and equipment to han-

dle small engines. Service procedures are given for those of you with the proper equipment to handle this operation.

1. Compress each valve spring and remove the valve keeper (**Figure 60**).

2. Remove the valve spring compressor, then the valve springs and valve components (refer to **Figure 61**, left to right: valve spring seat; outer spring; inner spring; top collar; valve; O-seal; and split collar).

3. Measure side clearance of each valve while it is positioned in the cylinder head, using a dial indicator. Refer to **Table 3** and replace any valve and/or its guide if clearance exceeds the service limits specified.

4. Measure valve stem diameter at 3 locations on the valve stem. Refer to **Table 4**. Replace

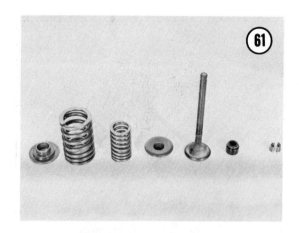

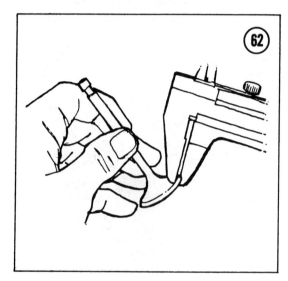

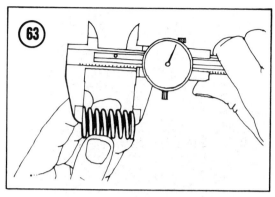

Table 3   VALVE STEM CLEARANCE

| Model | Service Limit | |
	Inches	Millimeters
250		
Intake	0.0032	0.08
Exhaust	0.0035	0.09
360		
Intake	0.0027	0.07
Exhaust	0.0035	0.09

Table 4   VALVE STEM SERVICE LIMITS

Model	Inches	Millimeters
250		
Intake	0.2738	6.95
Exhaust	0.2730	6.93
360		
Intake	0.2728	6.93
Exhaust	0.2728	6.93

Table 5   VALVE FACE WIDTH

Model	Standard Width	Service Limit
250 and 360	0.039-0.051 in. (1.0-1.3mm)	0.08 (2.0mm)

Table 6   VALVE SPRING FREE LENGTH

| Model | Service Limit | |
	Inches	Millimeters
250 and 360		
Outer	1.88	47.8
Inner	1.55	39.3

any valve if its stem is worn to less than the service limits specified.

NOTE: *When replacing valves, it is recommended that valve guides be replaced also. To do so, tap the guide from the cylinder head with a valve driving tool and a light hammer. Always install oversize guides when replacement is necessary, then ream to fit. Valve guide tools and reamers can be obtained through your Honda dealer.*

5. Measure width of each valve face as shown in **Figure 62**. Refer to **Table 5**. Grind valves to service limits specified.

6. Measure free length of each valve spring as shown in **Figure 63**. Refer to **Table 6**. Replace any valve spring with a free length shorter than that specified in the service limits.

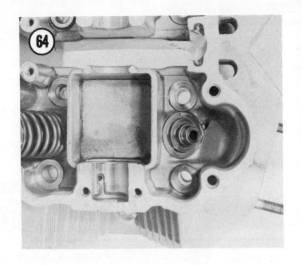

7. Install the valve seat (**Figure 64**). Then install the seal, springs, and top collar. Compress the springs with a valve spring compressor and install the keeper (**Figure 65**).

Cylinder Head Installation

1. Clean old gasket material from cylinder head and cylinder mating surfaces, and install a new gasket (coat the cylinder base with gasket cement). Set the cylinder head carefully in place and pull the cam chain up through the slot by the wire (**Figure 66**). Tighten all cylinder head bolts on 250 models to 13.0-14.5 ft.-lb. (180-200 cmkg); tighten cylinder head bolts on 360 models as follows: 6mm bolts, 5.1-8.0 ft.-lb. (0.7-1.1 mkg); and 10mm bolts, 21.7-24.6 ft.-lb. (3.0-3.4 mkg).

2. Install and tighten the 2 cylinder head mounting bolts to 6.2-7.2 ft.-lb. (60-75 cmkg). Refer to **Figure 67**.

3. Install the cam chain tensioner (**Figure 68**).

4. Install the front cam chain tensioner, then install the camshaft sprocket and loop the chain over it. Install the bolts loosely (the marks on the sprocket must be horizontal and the pin on the end of the camshaft must be pointing up). Refer to **Figure 69**.

5. Turn the alternator rotor with a wrench and align the LT mark with the timing mark on the housing (**Figure 70**).

6. Tighten the camshaft sprocket retaining bolts, then turn the sprocket to see if it rotates freely (**Figure 71**).

7. Install the oil seal (**Figure 72**).

CAUTION
Be sure that the thrust washer is in place (Figure 73).

8. Install the cylinder head cover and tighten the nuts evenly to 13.0-14.5 ft.-lb. (180-200 cmkg).

9. Install engine breather cover and gasket (refer to **Figure 74**).

10. Install spark advance mechanism and secure with center bolt (**Figure 75**).

NOTE: *Be sure to align the pins when installing the spark advance mechanism.*

4

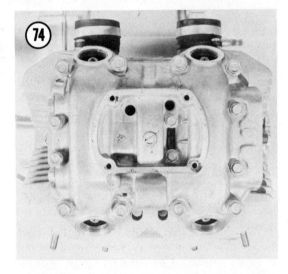

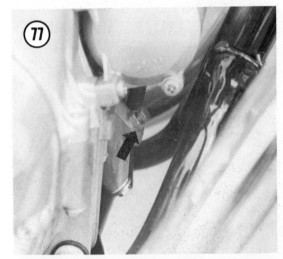

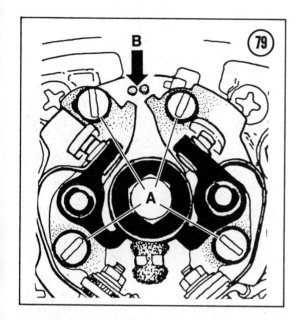

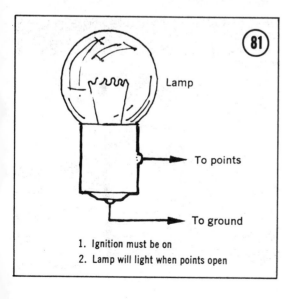

Lamp

→ To points

→ To ground

1. Ignition must be on
2. Lamp will light when points open

11. Install breaker point assembly with 2 screws (**Figure 76**).

12. Adjust the cam chain tension by loosening the locknut on the cam chain tensioner (**Figure 77**), backing off on the adjusting screw, and tightening it up again. Secure with the locknut.

13. Adjust the valve timing as described in the following procedure.

Breaker Point Adjustment

1. Turn engine over until one set of points is open to the maximum gap. Measure the breaker point gap with a feeler gauge (**Figure 78**). Point gap should be 0.012-0.016 in. (0.30-0.40mm).

2. If adjustment is necessary, slightly loosen the breaker point retaining screws (**Figure 79**) and insert a screwdriver into the pry slots, then move the stationary contact so that point gap is 0.014 in (0.35mm) as shown in **Figure 79**.

3. Tighten both retaining screws, then check gap again. Readjust if necessary.

4. Repeat preceding steps for remaining set of points.

5. Wipe the breaker cam clean, then apply a very small quantity of breaker cam lubricant. Apply just enough to create an oil film on the cam; more may cause point failure. This lubricant is sold at any auto parts store.

6. Place a wrench on the alternator bolt and turn the engine over until the LF mark on the alternator rotor aligns with the index pointer (**Figure 80**).

7. Connect a timing tester to the left-hand breaker point terminal and a good ground (follow the manufacture's hook-up instructions). If no timing tester is available, make up a test lamp as shown in **Figure 81**.

8. Loosen both of the left-hand points base plate retaining screws (**Figure 82**) just enough so that the base plate can be moved slightly.

9. Insert a screwdriver in the pry slots (refer to **Figure 82**) and rotate the base plate until the left-hand points just begin to open. (If a test lamp is used to determine point opening, be sure that ignition switch is ON.) The test lamp will light exactly at the moment that the LF mark on the alternator rotor aligns with the index pointer, if the ignition timing is correct.

4

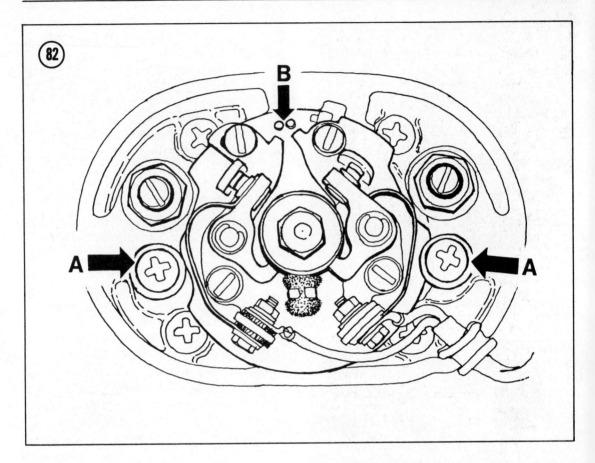

10. Tighten both base plate retaining screws (refer to **Figure 82**).

11. Recheck adjustment by turning rotor clockwise slightly, then counterclockwise slowly. The LF mark and index should align just as the left-hand points open (and the test lamp lights up). Readjust if necessary.

12. Turn rotor counterclockwise until F mark aligns with the index (**Figure 83**).

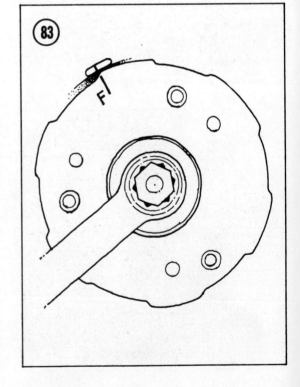

13. Connect the timing tester to the right-hand points.

14. Slightly loosen both right-hand stationary breaker contact retaining screws, then pry stationary contact slightly one way or the other until the points just begin to open.

> NOTE: *The point gap will change slightly; this is normal.*

15. Tighten both retaining screws.

16. Recheck adjustment by turning rotor clockwise slightly, then counterclockwise slowly. The right-hand points should open and the

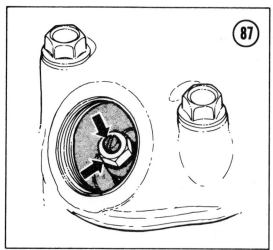

test lamp light up just as the F mark and index align. Readjust if necessary.

Valve Adjustment

Valves must be adjusted with the engine cold.

1. Remove tappet covers (**Figure 84**).

2. Place a wrench on the alternator rotor bolt and turn engine counterclockwise until left cylinder intake valve opens fully, then starts to close. Continue turning engine from this point until LT mark on alternator rotor aligns with the index pointer (**Figure 85**). Note that both valves for the left cylinder are fully closed at this point.

3. Insert a feeler gauge between tappet adjuster screw and valve stem. The intake valve clearance should be 0.002 in. (0.05mm), and the exhaust valve clearance 0.003 in. (0.08mm). See **Figure 86**.

4. If clearance is not correct, refer to **Figure 87**. Loosen locknut, then turn adjustment screw to produce a slight drag on the feeler gauge. Hold screw in position and tighten locknut.

> NOTE: *Clearance may change when locknut is tightened, so recheck adjustment and readjust if necessary.*

5. After both left cylinder valves are adjusted, turn engine counterclockwise (180 degrees) until T mark on rotor aligns with index. Adjust right cylinder valves (follow Steps 5 and 6, preceding).

6. Install tappet covers (refer to **Figure 84**).

CYLINDERS AND PISTONS

The cylinders are of cast lightweight aluminum alloy, and have cast iron liners of sufficient thickness to permit boring and honing after long usage or a piston seizure. Pistons are of lightweight aluminum alloy.

Cylinder Removal

1. Remove the cylinder head (refer to *Cylinder Head, Removal*, preceding section).
2. Lift the cylinders up and off of the crankcase (**Figure 88**).

> NOTE: *It may be necessary to tap the cylinders with a rubber or plastic mallet in order to remove them. If so, take care not to damage the cooling fins.*

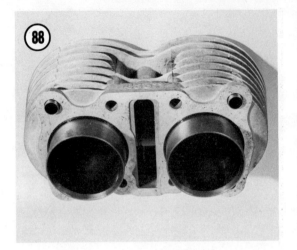

Checking Cylinders

Measure cylinder diameter at the top, middle, and bottom of each cylinder, using an accurate cylinder gauge. Measurements should be made both parallel and at a right angle to the crankshaft at each measurement depth. If any measurement exceeds the wear limit specified in **Table 7**, or if any 2 measurements differ by 0.002 in. (0.05mm), rebore and hone the cylinder to the next oversize. Pistons are available in oversizes of 0.25, 0.50, 0.75, and 1.00mm.

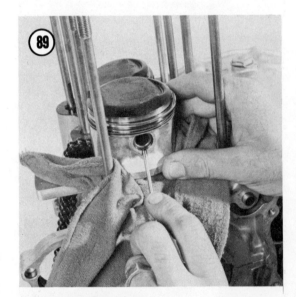

Piston Removal

1. Support the piston with a piece of wood. Remove the piston pin clip (stuff a clean shop cloth under the piston so the piston pin clip will not accidentally fall into the cylinder). See **Figure 89**.
2. Drive piston pin out (**Figure 90**) and remove the piston.

> NOTE: *If piston pin is a very tight fit, lay rags soaked in hot water around the piston. The pin will come out quite*

Table 7   CYLINDER WEAR LIMITS

Model	Inches	Millimeters
250	2.209	56.1
360	2.630	66.8

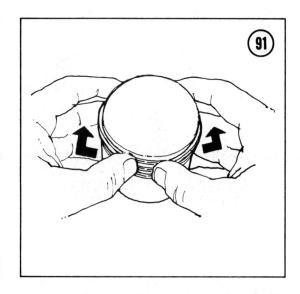

easily after a few moments. Wipe up any excess hot water with a soft, clean cloth.

Piston Ring Replacement

1. Spread the top piston ring with a thumb on each end of the ring, and remove it from the top of the piston. Take care not to scratch the piston. Repeat this procedure for each remaining ring. See **Figure 91**.

2. Scrape heavy carbon deposits from the piston head (**Figure 92**).

3. Clean carbon and gum from the piston ring grooves (**Figure 93**), using a broken ring. Any deposits remaining in ring grooves will cause replacement rings to stick, thereby causing gas blow-by and loss of power.

4. Measure piston rings for wear as shown in **Figure 94**. Insert each piston ring into the cylinder to a depth of 0.2 in. (5mm). To ensure that the ring is squarely in the cylinder, push it into position with the piston head. Standard gaps and wear limits are specified in **Table 8**. Replace all rings if any ring is worn so much that the piston ring gap exceeds the wear limit.

5. Before installing rings, check fit of each one in its groove. To do so, slip the outer surface of the ring into its groove, then roll the ring completely around the piston (**Figure 95**). If any binding occurs, determine and correct its cause before proceeding.

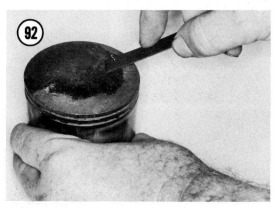

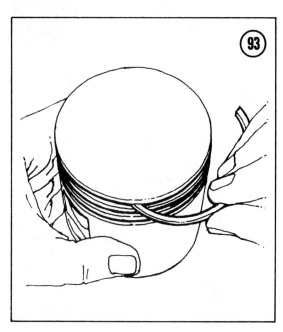

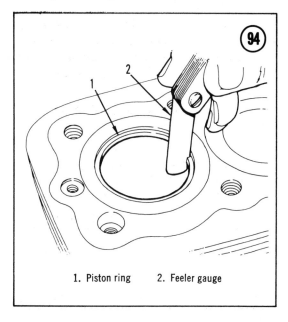

1. Piston ring   2. Feeler gauge

6. After installation, measure clearance between each ring and its groove at several places around the piston, as shown in **Figure 96**. Replace the ring and/or piston if ring groove clearance exceeds service limits specified in **Table 9**.

7. When replacing piston rings, install the lower one first. Be sure that they are installed so that all manufacturer's marks are toward the piston crown. If this precaution is not observed, oil pumping will occur. Position piston rings so that their gaps are staggered at 120 degree intervals (**Figure 97**).

Piston Clearance

Piston clearance is the difference between maximum piston diameter and minimum cylinder diameter. Measure piston diameter across the piston skirt (**Figure 98**) at right angles to the piston pin. Standard piston clearances and wear limits are listed in **Table 10**.

A piston showing signs of seizure will result in noise, loss of power, and cylinder wall damage. If such a piston is reused without correction, another seizure will develop. To correct this condition, lightly smooth the affected area with No. 400 emery paper or a fine oilstone. Replace any piston which is deeply scratched.

Piston Pins

Measure piston pin diameter at its center and at both ends. Also measure piston pin bore in its piston. Standard clearance should be 0.0001-0.0006 in. (0.002-0.014mm). Replace the pistons and/or piston pin if clearance exceeds 0.0047 in. (0.12mm).

Table 8   PISTON RING GAP

| Model | Standard Value | | Wear Limit | |
	Inches	Millimeters	Inches	Millimeters
250	0.006	0.15	0.029	0.75
360				
Top	0.008-0.016	0.20-0.40	0.031	0.80
Second	0.006-0.014	0.15-0.35	0.030	0.75
Oil	0.008-0.016	0.20-0.40	0.031	0.80

Table 9   PISTON RING GROOVE CLEARANCE

| Model | Standard Clearance | | Service Limit | |
	Inches	Millimeters	Inches	Millimeters
250				
Top	0.0012-0.0024	0.030-0.060	0.007	0.18
Second	0.0006-0.0018	0.015-0.045	0.006	0.16
Oil	0.0004-0.0018	0.010-0.045	0.007	0.17
360				
Top	0.0008-0.0024	0.020-0.060	0.006	0.15
Second	0.0008-0.0016	0.020-0.040	0.006	0.016
Oil	0.0004-0.0018	0.010-0.045	0.006	0.15

Table 10   PISTON CLEARANCE

| Model | Standard Clearance | | Wear Limit | |
	Inches	Millimeters	Inches	Millimeters
250 and 360	0.0008-0.0020	0.02-0.05	0.008	0.20

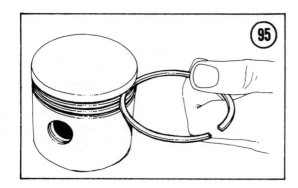

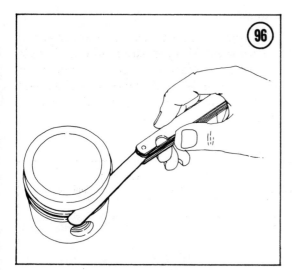

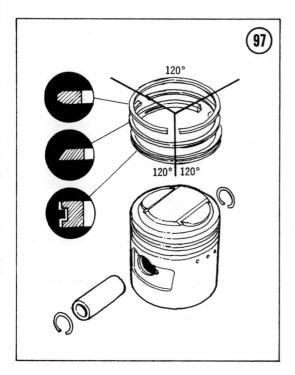

Piston Installation

1. Coat pistons with assembly oil and set in position over the connecting rods and insert the piston pins (if pins go in hard, soak pistons in hot water, the pin will push in easily. Wipe excess water off with a soft, clean cloth). Refer to **Figure 99**.

> NOTE: *The arrow on the piston should point toward the front of the engine.*

2. Install new piston pin clips (stuff a clean shop cloth under the piston to avoid losing the piston pin clip down into the cylinder). See **Figure 100**.

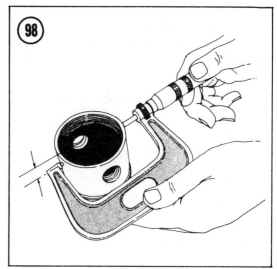

Cylinder Installation

1. Coat the cylinder bore with assembly oil.

2. Coat the cylinder base with gasket cement, then install a new gasket.

3. Set the cylinder carefully over the studs (**Figure 101**).

> CAUTION
> *Be sure that the cylinder locating dowels are in position (**Figure 102**).*

4. Gently depress the piston rings with a screwdriver (be careful not to nick the metal). See **Figure 103**.

5. Push the cylinder firmly down onto the crankcase (**Figure 104**).

6. Install 2 seals (**Figure 105**).

7. Install the cylinder head (refer to *Cylinder Head* section, earlier in this chapter).

CRANKCASE

Crankcases on all models split into upper and lower halves without special tools. It is necessary to split crankcase halves to service the crankshaft, transmission, internal shifter components, and kickstarter. Although details differ slightly between various models, the following service procedures are generally applicable to all models.

Disassembly

1. Remove the cylinder head, cylinders, and pistons, as outlined previously.

2. Remove bolt shown in **Figure 106**.

3. Remove ten 6mm and nine 8mm bolts (**Figure 107**), then tap crankcase with a rubber or plastic mallet to loosen it, and lift it off. **Figure 108** shows the bottom half of the crankcase containing the crankshaft and transmission.

> CAUTION
> *Do not pry or use any metal tool to separate the 2 crankcase halves. Mating surfaces may be damaged, resulting in oil leakage.*

Inspection

Lubricating oil passages are machined in the crankcase. Be very careful that these passages

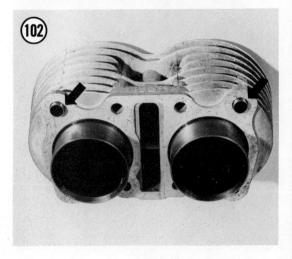

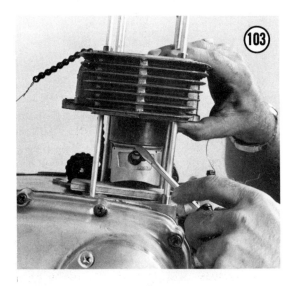

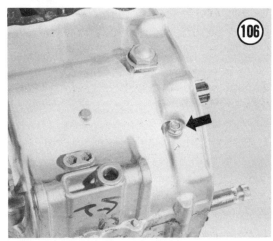

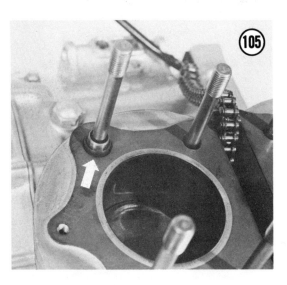

do not become clogged during service operations. If any passage is clogged, blow it out with compressed air. Examine mating surfaces of both halves for nicks or scratches which will result in oil leaks. Clean off all traces of old sealing compound.

Reassembly

1. Be sure that mating surfaces of both crankcase halves are clean.

2. Coat mating surfaces with liquid gasket compound (**Figure 109**).

CAUTION

Do not get gasket compound on dowel pins or surfaces which do not mate. (Be sure that these dowel pins are in position when reassembling the 2 crankcase halves — refer to Figure 109).

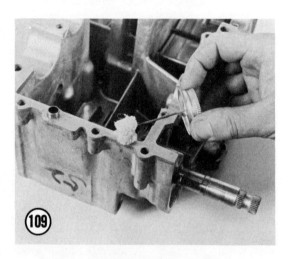

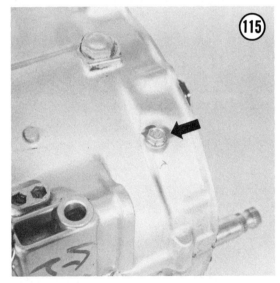

3. Reassemble both crankcase halves (**Figure 110**) and install bolts loosely (**Figure 111**).

4. Be sure oil seals are in place (**Figure 112**).

5. Turn crankshaft and transmission shaft to be sure it is not binding (**Figure 113**).

> NOTE: *If there is binding (refer to Step 5, preceding), it is possible that the cam chain tensioning spring is not fully depressed and locked. Disassemble the 2 crankcase halves again and check the tensioner. (The flat on the cam chain tensioner shaft should align with the bolt, as shown in* **Figure 114**).

6. Tighten the crankcase 8mm bolts to 11.5-12.2 ft.-lb. (1.6-1.7 mkg); the 6mm bolts to 5.8-6.5 ft.-lb. (0.8-0.9 mkg). Refer to **Figure 111**.

7. Install and tighten the bolt shown in **Figure 115**.

CRANKSHAFT

The crankshaft operates under conditions of high stress. Dimensional tolerances are critical. It is necessary to locate and correct crankshaft defects early to prevent more serious troubles later.

Removal

1. Split the crankcase halves (refer to *Crankcase* section, preceding).

2. Lift out the cam chain tensioner guide (**Figure 116**) and remove the crankshaft.

Inspection

Measurement locations and support points are shown in **Figure 117**. Replace the crankshaft if runout exceeds 0.118 in. (3.0mm) at locations C, D, E, or F. Maximum runout tolerance at locations A or B is 0.006 in. (0.15mm).

Installation

1. To install the crankshaft, reverse the *Removal* procedure, and observe the following notes:

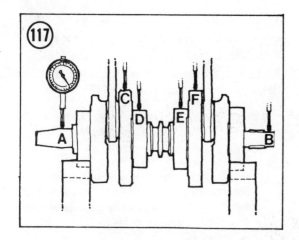

a. The 2 dowels on the center main bearing, and the indentation shown in **Figure 118** must align with the slots in the center main bearing housing and the dowel in the left main bearing housing as shown in **Figure 119**.

b. Set the crankshaft in position as shown in **Figure 120**. Let the cam chain drop down through the opening in the crankcase. (Stretch it fairly taut, then tie it to a stud after looping it over the sprocket on the crankshaft. This will prevent the chain from slipping off the crankshaft sprocket during further engine reassembly.)

c. Install the cam chain tensioner guide **(Figure 116)**.

2. Reassemble the crankcase halves (refer to *Crankcase* section, preceding).

TRANSMISSION

Removal

1. Split the crankcase and remove the crankshaft as outlined in preceding sections.

2. Lift out the input shaft **Figure 121** and output shaft **(Figure 122)**.

Inspection

1. Measure backlash between each pair of gears. Replace the gears in pairs if the backlash exceeds 0.008 in. (0.2mm).

2. Check gear teeth for wear, nicks, or burrs. Minor defects may be smoothed with an oil-stone. If one gear requires replacement, it is good practice to replace its mating gear also.

3. Be sure that sliding gears move smoothly along their splines, with no excessive looseness.

4. Check dog clutches for tooth wear. Worn clutch teeth may result in noise or jumping out of gear.

5. Place gears in neutral. Check that there is no interference between dog clutches and adjacent gears.

6. For more detailed inspection, the input shaft comes apart in the sequence shown in **Figure 123**; **Figure 124** shows the input shaft assembled.

7. The output shaft comes apart in the sequence shown in **Figure 125; Figure 126** shows the output shaft assembled.

8. The oil pump comes apart in the sequence shown in **Figure 127**.

9. The kickstarter comes apart in the sequence shown in **Figure 128**.

10. The chain adjuster is shown unassembled in **Figure 129**.

11. **Figure 130** shows the unassembled shifter forks and shift drum.

Installation

1. Install the kickstarter in the crankcase as shown in **Figure 131** (engaged) **and 132** (disengaged).

2. Install new O-rings before you install the oil pump (**Figure 133**).

3. Install the oil pump (**Figure 134**).

4. Install the cam chain tensioner so that the flat spot on the shaft is aligned with the bolt (**Figure 135**).

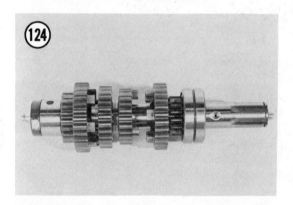

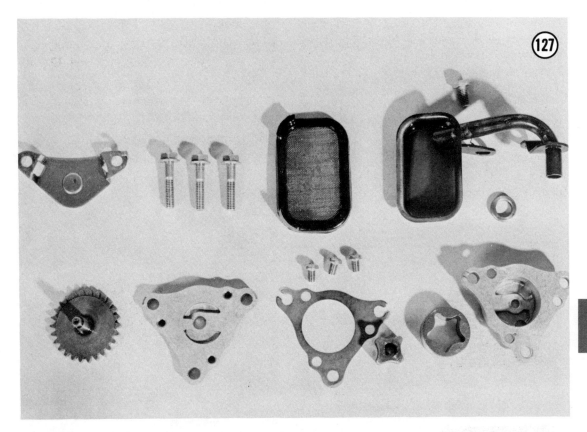

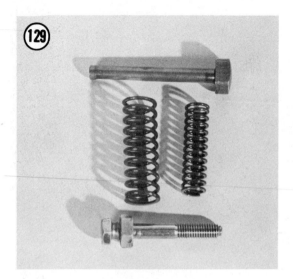

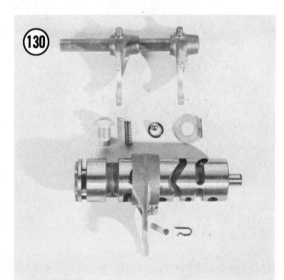

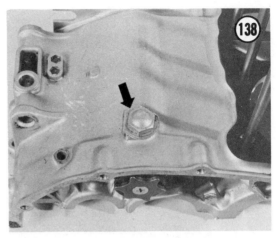

5. Install 2 rear shifter forks on shifter shaft **(Figure 136)**.

6. Install shifter drum with remaining center shifter fork and insert guide pin in slot and secure with guide pin clip **(Figure 137)**.

7. Install shift drum ball detent (ball bearing, spring, and plunger). Turn shift shaft while looking down into the bolt hole in order to find the detent. Tighten the shift drum retaining bolt and install the safety tab **(Figure 138)**.

8. Be sure the bearing retainer (left side of crankcase housing) and the dowel (right side of crankcase housing) are in place **(Figure 139)**.

9. Install the transmission input shaft (be sure dowel pin is aligned with the bearing outer race, and that the groove in the bearing sets over the bearing retainer **(Figure 140)**.

10. Install the transmission output shaft (take same precaution as in Step 9, preceding). See **Figure 141**.

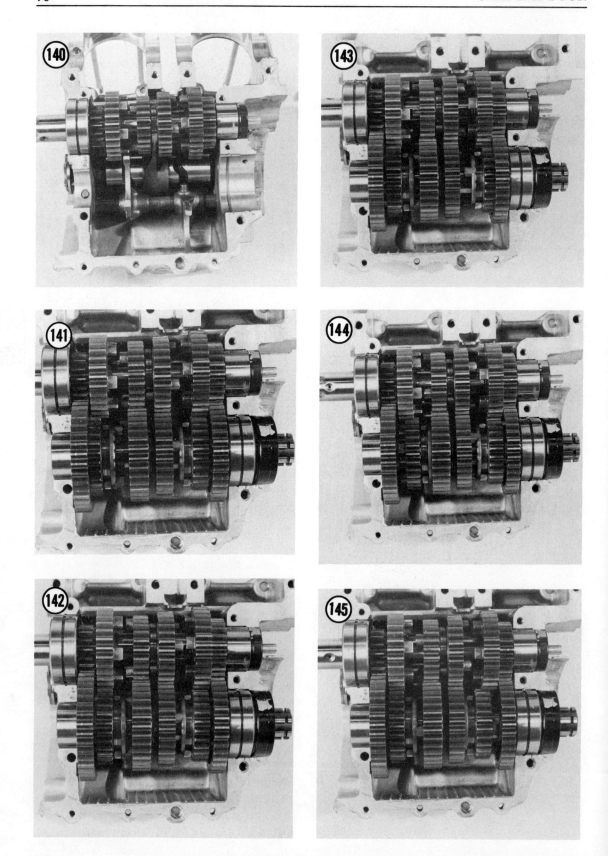

NOTE: *Turn the shafts to be sure everything rotates freely.*

11. The transmission is shown in first gear in **Figure 142**; neutral, **Figure 143**; second, **Figure 144**; third, **Figures 145**; fourth, **Figure 146**; and fifth, **Figure 147**.

12. Install the crankshaft and reassemble the 2 crankcase halves as outlined in the previous sections.

FINAL ENGINE REASSEMBLY

1. Install starter sprocket and sprocket retaining plate and bolt (**Figure 148**).

2. Install rotor and retaining bolt (**Figure 149**).

3. Lay the starter chain and small sprocket in place (**Figure 150**), then install starter and secure with mounting bolts (**Figure 151**).

4. Install gasket and side cover (install long and short bolts as shown in **Figure 152**).

5. Install detent stopper plate (**Figure 153**), shifter shaft (**Figure 154**), and kickstarter spring (**Figure 155**). Then wind the kickstarter spring around until the end of it is captured by the lug on the casing. Install a plain washer and snap ring (**Figure 156**).

CLUTCH AND OIL PUMP

Installation

1. Install sprocket and clutch housing (**Figure 157**).

2. Install clutch hub and clutch hub snap ring (**Figure 158**).

3. Install push crown (**Figure 159**).

> NOTE: *Be sure push crown engages with rounded end of pushrod.*

4. Install all clutch friction and steel plates as a unit (**Figure 160**).

> NOTE: *After you install the initial friction plate, install a steel plate, friction plate, steel plate, etc. You will end up with a friction plate on the outside.*

5. Install the pressure plate, clutch springs, and hex bolts (**Figure 161**).

> NOTE: *Tighten each hex nut a little bit at a time to equalize pressure.*

6. Tighten hex bolts in clutch pressure plate. (Place a rag between the gears to keep gears from turning. To remove the rag, reverse the direction of the gears.) See **Figure 162**.

7. Install the centrifugal oil filter as follows:

    a. Install cupped washer (it is marked OUTSIDE), then the lockwasher and nut.

    b. Tighten the nut with a special Honda wrench, available at your Honda dealer. **Figure 163** shows the nut and the special tool.

8. Install oil filter end cap and oil filter end cap snap ring (**Figure 164**).

9. Install oil pump drive gear (**Figure 165**).

10. Install gasket and side cover (all bolts are the same length). See **Figure 166**.

ENGINE INSTALLATION

1. Set engine into frame.

2. Lift engine slightly, then install lower engine mounting bolts (**Figure 167**, front; **Figure 168**, rear).

3. Install top rear engine mounting bolt (**Figure 169**).

4. Insert tachometer cable into tachometer housing and install retaining screw (**Figure 170**).

5. Connect wiring harness to frame with frame clips.

6. Install spark plug wires.

7. Connect breaker point wire.

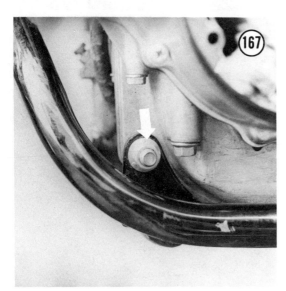

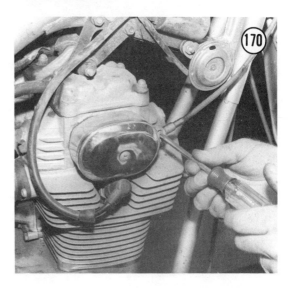

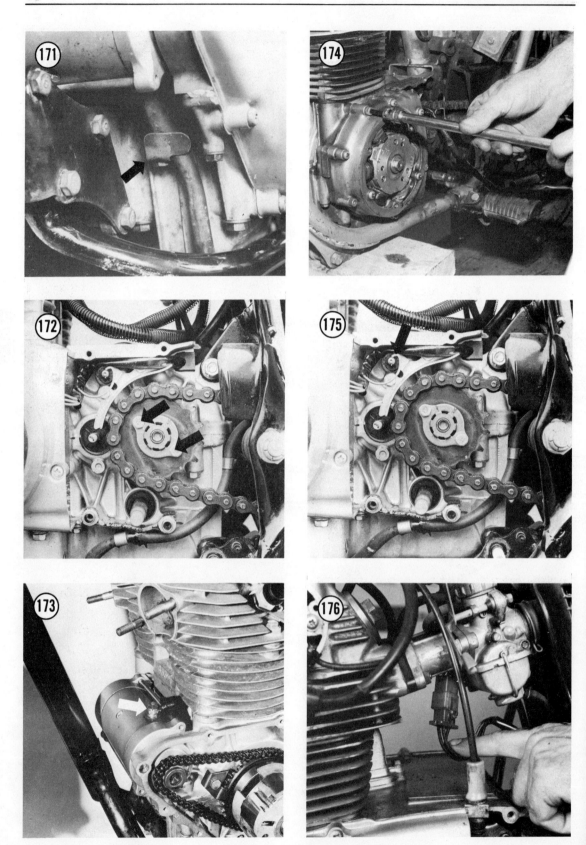

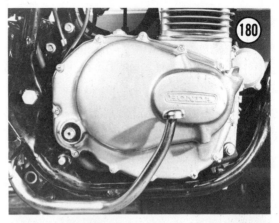

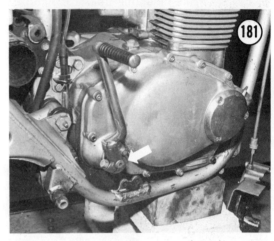

4

8. Install starter cable retaining clips (**Figure 171**).

9. Install sprocket and sprocket retaining bolts (**Figure 172**).

10. Connect starter cable (**Figure 173**).

11. Install alternator housing (**Figure 174**).

12. Install neutral light switch (**Figure 175**).

13. Connect electrical plug (**Figure 176**).

14. Install alternator cover (**Figure 177**).

15. Connect clutch cable (**Figure 178**).

16. Install cover (**Figure 179**).

17. Install case (**Figure 180**).

> NOTE: *Be sure that thrust washer is installed on shaft.*

18. Install kickstarter (**Figure 181**).

19. Install footrests (**Figure 182**).

20. Install carburetors on cylinder heads with retaining nuts (**Figure 183**). Engage throttle

cables in all routing clamps and connect push-pull throttle cables to the twist grip.

21. Install air filters with 2 retaining bolts (each filter) and tighten the air filter clamp screw (**Figures 184, 185, and 186**).

22. Install gas tank.

23. Connect battery cable.

24. Connect fuel lines to fuel petcock.

25. Install engine drain plug and fill with engine oil.

Final Checks

1. Check engine mounting bolts for tightness as a final precaution.

2. Adjust the clutch, throttle cable, drive chain, ignition timing, and valves (refer to Chapter Two for procedures).

3. Inspect all nuts and bolts for tightness.

4. Check wiring for chafing or binding after engine installation.

5. Start engine and check for oil or fuel leaks.

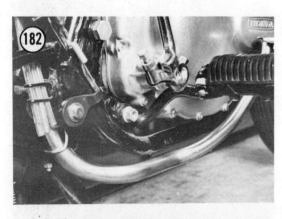

CHAPTER FIVE

FUEL AND EXHAUST SYSTEMS

For proper operation, a gasoline engine must be supplied with fuel and air, mixed in proper proportions by weight. A mixture in which there is excess fuel is said to be rich. A lean mixture is one which contains insufficient fuel. It is the function of the carburetor to supply proper mixture to the engine under all operating conditions.

The Honda twins covered in this manual use vacuum piston carburetors (the slide position is controlled by engine vacuum).

CARBURETOR OVERHAUL

There is no set rule regarding frequency of carburetor overhaul. A carburetor used on a machine used primarily for street riding may go 5,000 miles without attention. If the machine is used in dirt, the carburetor might need an overhaul in less than 1,000 miles. Poor engine performance, hesitation, and little or no response to idle mixture adjustment are all symptoms of possible carburetor malfunctions.

Removal/Installation

1. Remove the clamps and retaining nuts and lift the air cleaner (one on each side) off (**Figure 1 and 2**).

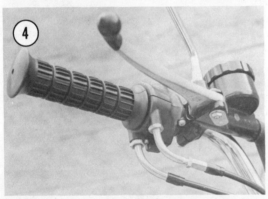

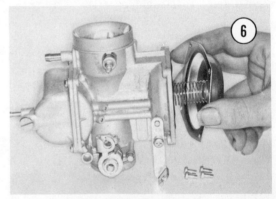

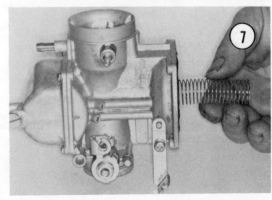

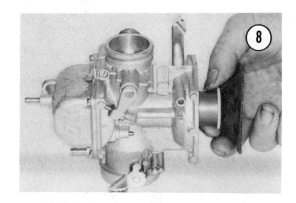

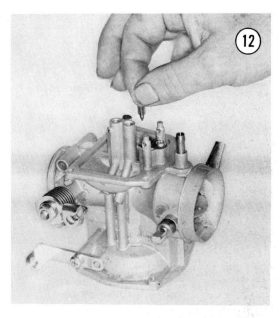

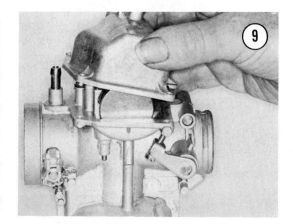

2. Remove carburetor clamps and intake hoses (**Figure 3**).

3. Disconnect throttle cables from throttle twist grip and loosen all routing clamps (**Figure 4**).

4. Remove carburetor assembly (with cables attached). See **Figure 5**.

5. Installation is the reverse of the preceding steps.

Disassembly/Assembly

1. Remove 4 retaining screws, then pull off the diaphragm (**Figure 6**).

2. Pull out diaphragm return spring (**Figure 7**).

3. Pull out diaphragm and slide as an assembly (**Figure 8**). Note the locating tab on the diaphragm near the throttle cable bracket.

4. Remove the 4 screws, then the float bowl (**Figure 9**).

5. Pull out the main jet and pilot jet together by pulling on their retainer (**Figure 10**). Although these 2 jets appear to be similar, they may be distinguished by size; the main jet is larger. Always replace O-rings upon reassembly.

6. Remove the float assembly by pulling out its pivot shaft (**Figure 11**).

7. Remove the float needle (**Figure 12**).

8. Using needle nose pliers with *taped* jaws,

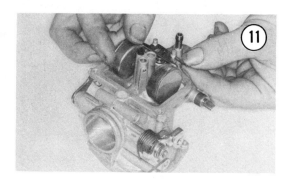

Table 1   CARBURETOR ADJUSTMENT SUMMARY

Throttle Opening	Adjustment	If too Rich	If too Lean
0 - 1/8	Air screw	Turn out	Turn in
1/8 - 1/4	Throttle valve cutaway	Use larger cutaway	Use smaller cutaway
1/4 - 3/4	Jet needle	Raise clip	Lower clip
3/4 - full	Main jet	Use smaller number	Use larger number

Table 2   CARBURETOR FLOAT HEIGHT

Model	Inches	Millimeters
250 and 360	0.75	19.0

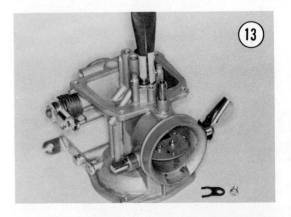

pull out the float needle valve seat, after first removing its retaining clip (**Figure 13**).

9. Push out the needle jet and slow speed jet, using a fiber or plastic tool (**Figure 14**).

10. Remove the idle mixture screw and its spring (**Figure 15**).

11. Remove the drain plug (**Figure 16**).

12. The slide and diaphragm assembly may be disassembled by compressing the jet needle retaining clip with a pair of long nose pliers.

13. Reverse the preceding steps to reassemble the carburetor. Always use new gaskets and O-rings upon reassembly. Be sure to check float level before returning carburetor to service (refer to *Carburetor Adjustment* in the following section).

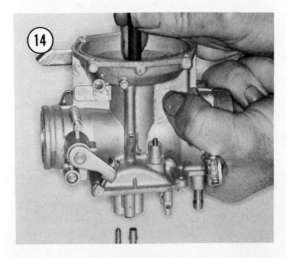

CARBURETOR ADJUSTMENT

The carburetor was designed to provide the proper mixture under all operation conditions. Little or no benefit will result from experimenting. However, unusual operating conditions such as sustained operation at high altitudes or unusually high or low temperatures may make modifications to standard specifications desirable. The adjustments described in the following paragraphs should only be undertaken if the rider has definite reason to believe they are required. Make the tests and adjustments in the order specified. Float level should be checked each time the carburetor is disassembled, and adjusted if necessary.

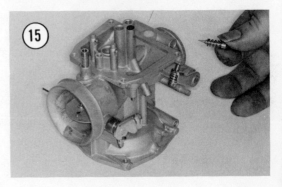

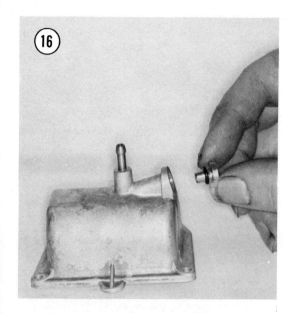

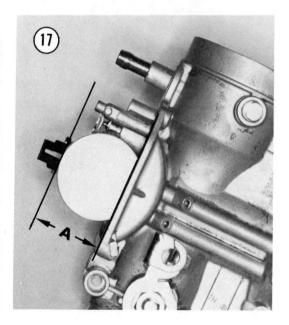

BEND TANG
TO ADJUST
FLOAT LEVEL

A summary of carburetor adjustments is given in **Table 1**.

Float Level

To check carburetor float level, refer to **Figure 17**.

1. Tilt the carburetor slowly until the tang on the float just barely touches the float needle.

2. Measure the distance between the bottom of the float and the bottom surface of the carburetor body (**Figure 17**). This distance must be as specified in **Table 2**, and equal for both floats. Bend the tang on the float arm (**Figure 18**) as necessary if adjustment is required.

Jet Size

Make a road test at full throttle for final determination of main jet size. To make such a test, operate the motorcycle at full throttle for at least two minutes, then shut the engine off, release the clutch, and bring the machine to a stop.

If at full throttle, the engine runs "heavily," the main jet is too large. If the engine runs better by closing the throttle slightly, the main jet is too small. The engine will run at full throttle evenly and regularly if the main jet is of the correct size.

After each such test, remove and examine the spark plugs. The insulators should have a light tan color. If the insulators have black sooty deposits, the mixture is too rich. If there are signs of intense heat, such as a blistered white appearance, the mixture is too lean.

As a general rule, main jet size should be reduced approximately 5 percent for each 3,000 feet (1,000 meters) above sea level.

Table 3 lists symptoms caused by rich and lean mixtures.

Idle Speed and Mixture Adjustment

1. Start engine and allow it to warm to operating temperature, then shut it off.

2. Turn each idle mixture screw in until it seats lightly, then back out each one 1¼ turns (**Figure 19**).

3. Start the engine. Adjust each idle speed screw so that the engine idles at 1,000-2,000 rpm (**Figure 20**).

5

Table 3   POOR MIXTURE SYMPTOMS

Condition	Symptom
Rich mixture	Rough idle
	Black exhaust smoke
	Hard starting, especially when hot
	Black deposits in exhaust pipes
	Gas-fouled spark plugs
	Poor gas mileage
	Engine performs worse as it warms up
Lean mixture	Backfiring
	Rough idle
	Overheating
	Hesitation upon acceleration
	Engine speed varies at fixed throttle
	Loss of power
	White color on spark plug insulators
	Poor acceleration

Table 4   CARBURETOR JETS

Model	Pilot Jet	Main Jet
250	35	68 (primary); 95 (secondary)
360	35	68 (primary); 68 (secondary)

4. Place one hand behind each muffler and adjust idle speed screw (refer to **Figure 20**) until exhaust pressure from each muffler is equal.

5. Turn left cylinder idle mixture screw in either direction, slowly, until engine idle speed is at its maximum.

6. Repeat Step 5 for the right cylinder.

7. Check exhaust pressure from each cylinder (as in Step 4) and adjust either idle speed screw necessary to equalize pressures.

8. Turn each idle speed screw an equal amount to obtain 1,000-1,200 rpm idle speed.

If the preceding procedure does not work well, due to both carburetors being too far out of adjustment, use the following procedure:

1. Turn the idle mixture screw on each carburetor in until it seats lightly, then back it out 1¼ turns (refer to **Figure 19**).

2. Start the engine, then ride the bike long enough to warm it thoroughly.

3. Stop the engine and disconnect either spark plug lead (**Figure 21**).

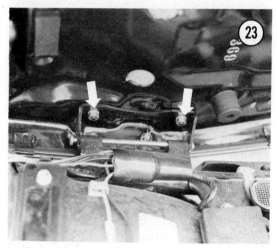

10. Start the engine, then turn each idle speed screw an equal amount until the engine idles at 1,000-1,200 rpm.

11. Place one hand behind each muffler and check that the exhaust pressures are equal (**Figure 22**). If not, turn either idle speed screw in or out until they are.

MISCELLANEOUS CARBURETOR PROBLEMS

Water in carburetor float bowls can result from careless washing of the motorcycle. To remedy the problem, remove and clean the carburetor bowl, main jet, and any other affected parts. Be sure to cover the air intake when washing the machine.

If gasoline leaks past the float bowl gasket, high speed fuel starvation may occur. Varnish deposits on the outside of the float bowl are evidence of this condition.

Dirt in the fuel may lodge in the float valve and cause an overrich mixture. As a temporary measure, tap the carburetor lightly with any convenient tool to dislodge the dirt. Clean the fuel tank, petcock, fuel line, and carburetor at the first opportunity, should this situation occur.

CARBURETOR SPECIFICATIONS

Table 4 lists major specifications of carburetors of the more popular bikes covered by this manual. These specifications have been determined by exhaustive factory tests, and should not be changed unless there is good reason for doing so.

FUEL TANK

Removal/Installation

1. Loosen seat mounting bolts, then remove the seat (**Figure 23**).

2. Be sure that the fuel flow is shut off at the petcock, then remove fuel line(s) at petcock (**Figure 24**).

3. Detach fuel tank from its rear rubber mount; lift it upward and to the rear. Be sure that no wires catch on the tank as it is removed (**Figure 25**).

4. Restart the engine on one cylinder. Turn the idle speed screw on the "working" carburetor in enough to keep the engine running (refer to **Figure 20**).

5. Turn the idle speed screw out until the engine runs slower and begins to falter.

6. Turn the idle mixture screw in or out to make the engine run smoothly. Note the speed indicated by the tachometer.

7. Repeat Steps 5 and 6 to achieve the lowest possible stable idle speed.

8. Stop the engine, then reconnect the spark plug lead that was disconnected.

9. Repeat Steps 3 through 8 for the other cylinder, matching the engine speed with that observed in Step 6.

5

4. Reverse preceding steps to install the fuel tank.

Inspection

1. Be sure that the filler cap vent is not clogged.

2. Check all rubber mounts, and replace them if they are damaged.

3. Check fuel lines for leaks, hardening, or cracks.

4. Check for sediment in the tank, and flush out if necessary.

> WARNING
> *Open flames, cigarettes, water heater or clothes dryer pilot lights, or electrical sparks may trigger a fatal explosion. Do not work on any fuel system component within 50 feet of any possible source of ignition.*

Fuel Strainer Service

The fuel strainer filters out particles which might otherwise get into a carburetor and cause the float needle valve to remain open, resulting in flooding. Such particles might also get into the engine and cause damage.

Remove the fuel strainer, located at the fuel petcock (refer to **Figure 24**), and clean it in solvent, then blow dry with compressed air. Be sure that all gaskets are in good condition upon reassembly.

EXHAUST SYSTEM

Removal/Installation

1. Remove nuts at each cylinder head (**Figure 26**).

2. Remove footpegs and footrest bar if necessary (**Figure 27**).

3. Remove rear attachment bolts (**Figure 28**).

4. Reverse preceding steps to install the exhaust system.

Inspection

1. Check gaskets and rubber cushions for cracks or damage.

2. Pull out baffle tubes (if so equipped) and remove carbon deposits.

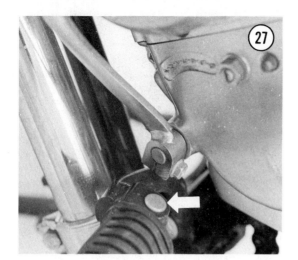

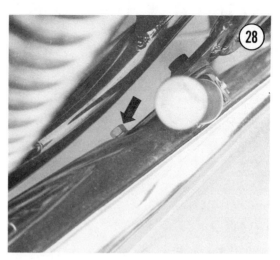

5

CHAPTER SIX

ELECTRICAL SYSTEM

This chapter covers operating principles and removal and installation procedures for Honda ignition and electrical systems. Refer to Chapter Two for tune-up procedures; refer to Chapter Three for troubleshooting procedures.

IGNITION SYSTEM

Honda twin-cylinder models are equipped with a battery and coil ignition system, similar in many ways to a conventional automobile.

Circuit Operation

Figure 1 illustrates a typical battery ignition system for a single cylinder. When the breaker points are closed, current flows from the battery through the primary windings of the ignition coil, thereby building a magnetic field around the coil. The breaker cam rotates at one-half crankshaft speed and is so adjusted that the breaker points open as the piston reaches firing position.

As the points open, the magnetic field collapses. When this happens, a very high voltage is induced (up to approximately 15,000 volts) in the secondary winding of the ignition coil. This high voltage is sufficient to jump the gap at the spark plug.

The condenser assists the coil in developing high voltage, and also protects the points. Inductance of the ignition coil primary winding tends to keep a surge of current flowing through the circuit even after the points have started to open. The condenser stores this surge and thus prevents arcing at the points. This circuit is duplicated for each cylinder.

Troubleshooting

Refer to Chapter Three, for any problems related to the electrical system.

Ignition Coil

The ignition coil is a transformer which develops the high voltage required to jump the spark plug gap. The only maintenance required is that of keeping the electrical connections clean and tight, and occasionally checking to see that the coil is mounted securely (**Figure 2**).

Service

There are two major items requiring service on battery ignition models: breaker point service and ignition timing. Both are vitally important to proper engine operation and reliability. Refer to Chapter Two, *Breaker Points* and *Ignition Timing* sections.

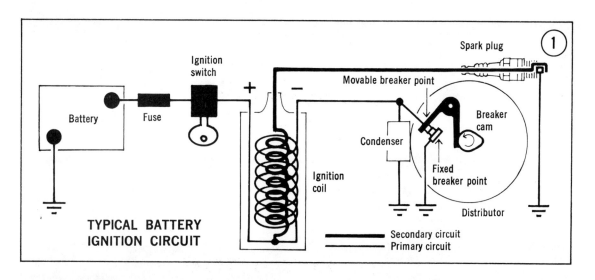

TYPICAL BATTERY IGNITION CIRCUIT

CHARGING SYSTEM

The charging system on all Honda twins covered by this manual consists of an alternator, battery, and interconnecting wiring. Some models are also equipped with a solid state voltage regulator.

Alternator

An alternator is an alternating current electrical generator in which a magnetized field rotor revolves within a set of stationary coils called a stator. As the rotor revolves, alternating current is induced in the stator. Stator current is then rectified and used to operate electrical accessories on the motorcycle and for battery charging. Refer to **Figure 3**.

Removal/Installation

1. Remove shift lever (**Figure 4**).

2. Remove alternator cover screws (**Figure 5**)

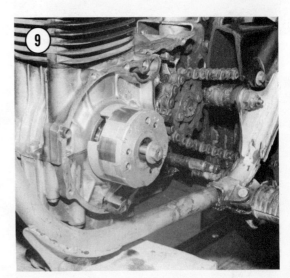

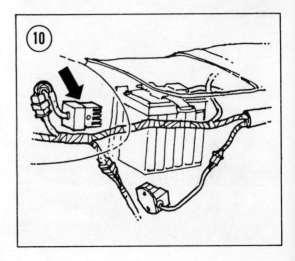

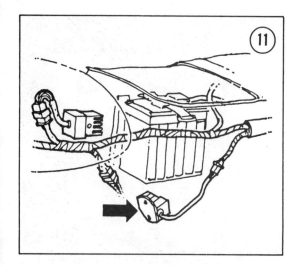

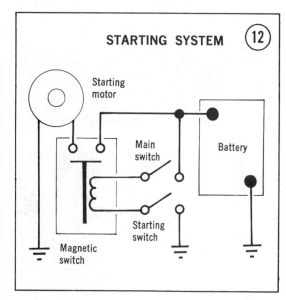

STARTING SYSTEM 12

Starting motor

Main switch

Battery

Starting switch

Magnetic switch

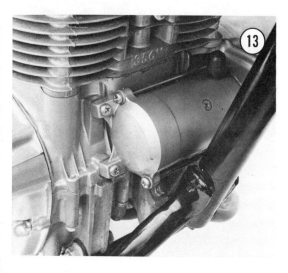

and tap cover off with a rubber mallet (**Figure 6**).

3. Remove clip holding alternator main wiring harness (**Figure 7**).

4. Remove neutral indicator switch (**Figure 8**).

5. Remove alternator retaining nut and pull alternator with a suitable puller (**Figure 9**).

6. Install by reversing the preceding steps.

Rectifier

All models are equipped with a full-wave bridge rectifier (**Figure 10**).

> *CAUTION*
> *Always handle the rectifier assembly carefully. Do not bend or try to rotate the wafers. Do not loosen the screws which hold the assembly together. Moisture can damage the assembly, so keep it dry. Never run the engine with the battery disconnected or without a fuse; doing so can cause immediate rectifier destruction.*

Voltage Regulator

Problems with this unit rarely occur. Refer to Chapter Three for test procedures for the voltage regulator should this unit be suspected of causing trouble (**Figure 11**).

> CAUTION
> *Do not connect or disconnect the regulator with the engine running.*

ELECTRIC STARTER

Refer to **Figure 12** for a diagram of a typical starting system.

Starter Motor

The starter motor (**Figure 13**) is wound in series for high torque, and draws approximately 120 amperes under normal starting conditions. This figure can vary considerably, depending on engine temperature, starter condition, and other factors.

Removal/Installation

1. Remove shift lever (**Figure 14**).

2. Remove alternator cover screws (**Figure 15**) and tap cover off with a rubber mallet (**Figure 16**).

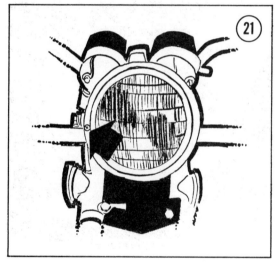

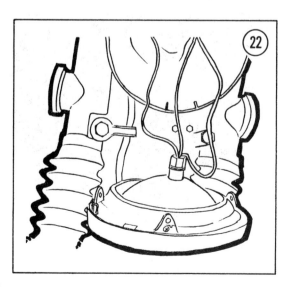

3. Remove starter motor retaining screws (**Figure 17**) and tap starter motor out of case (rearward) with a rubber mallet (**Figure 18**).

4. Remove chain and sprocket (**Figure 19**).

5. Remove starter sprocket setting plate (**Figure 20**), then remove starter sprocket (if necessary).

6. Install by reversing the preceding steps.

LIGHTS

The headlight assembly consists primarily of a headlight lens and reflector unit, rim, and related hardware.

In the event of lighting problems, first check the affected bulb. Poor ground connections are another cause of lamp malfunctions.

Turn signals usually operate from direct current supplied by the battery. When replacing the signal bulbs, always be sure to use the proper type. Erratic operation or even failure to flash may result from use of wrong bulbs.

Stoplights usually operate from direct current also. Stoplight switches should be adjusted so that the lamp comes on just before braking action begins. Front brake stoplight switches are frequently built into the front brake cable, and are not adjustable.

HEADLIGHT

Replacement

Refer to **Figure 21**.

1. Remove 3 screws and remove headlight from case.

2. Disconnect socket from sealed beam.

3. Remove 2 retaining lock pins and screws from rim.

4. Remove sealed beam.

5. Installation is the reverse of these steps. Adjust headlight as described below.

Adjustment

Adjust headlight horizontally and vertically, according to Department of Motor Vehicle regulations in your state.

To adjust headlight horizontally, turn the screw illustrated in **Figure 22**. To adjust vertically, loosen the bolts on either side of the

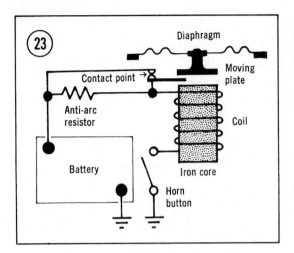

Diaphragm

Contact point →

Moving plate

Anti-arc resistor

Coil

Battery

Iron core

Horn button

case. Move the headlight to the desired position, then tighten bolts.

TAIL/STOPLIGHTS

Taillight Replacement

A single bulb performs as a taillight, license plate light, and stoplight. To replace the bulb, remove the lens and turn bulb counterclockwise.

HORN

Figure 23 is a typical horn circuit. Current for the horn is supplied by the battery. One terminal is connected to the battery through the main switch. The other terminal is grounded when the horn button is pressed.

BATTERY SERVICE

Honda motorcycles are equipped with lead-acid storage batteries, smaller in size but similar in construction, to batteries used in automobiles **(Figure 24)**.

Refer to Chapter Two, *Battery* section, for maintenance procedures.

WIRING DIAGRAMS

Reference to the following wiring diagrams will make electrical system troubleshooting easier. Diagrams of all models available are included.

Refer to Chapter Three for troubleshooting procedures.

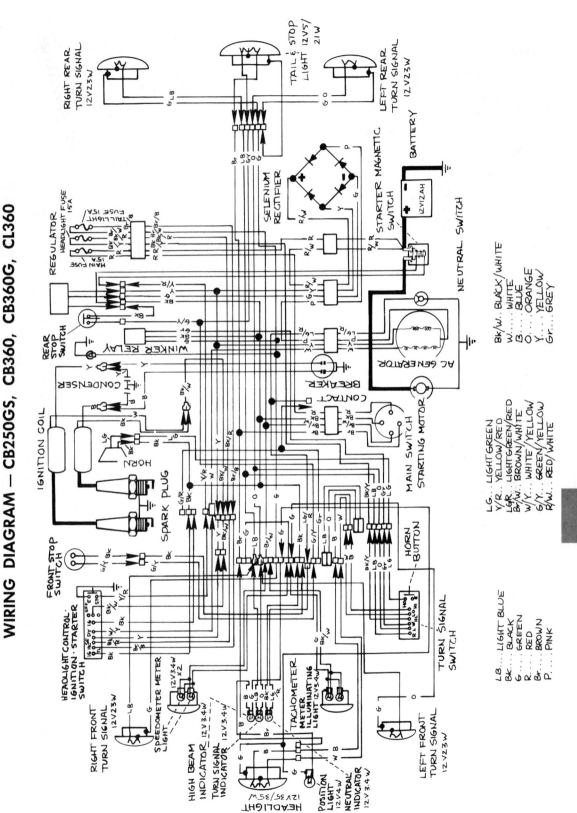

WIRING DIAGRAM — CB250GS, CB360, CB360G, CL360

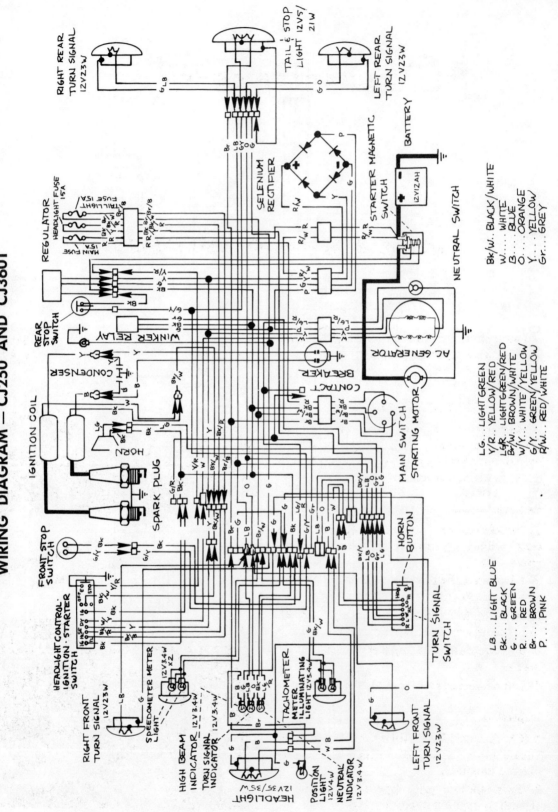

WIRING DIAGRAM — CJ250 AND CJ360T

FRAME, SUSPENSION, AND STEERING

This chapter provides all service procedures for the wheels, brakes, chassis, and related components.

HANDLEBAR

Most manual controls are mounted on the handlebar assembly. Wiring from switches is routed to the headlight, where it is connected to the main wiring harness.

Removal

1. Disconnect front brake cable (**Figure 1**) and clutch cables (**Figure 2**) at their respective levers.
2. Disconnect the throttle cable at the throttle grip (**Figure 3**).
3. Remove the headlight assembly (**Figure 4**), then disconnect all wiring from the handlebar.
4. Remove bolts and handlebar clamps (**Figure 5**).
5. Lift handlebar from fork top bridge.

Inspection

1. Check cables for chafed or kinked housings. Grease inner cables and be sure that cables operate smoothly.
2. Twist throttle grip. Operation should be smooth throughout its entire travel.

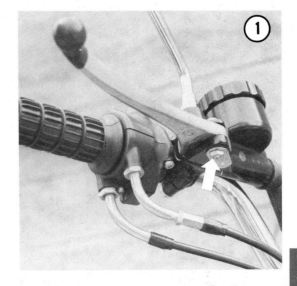

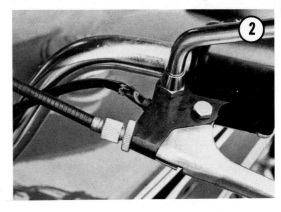

7

3. Check both hand levers for smooth operation.

4. Check handlebar tubing for cracks or bends.

5. Check switches for proper operation.

6. Inspect wiring for chafed or frayed insulation. Be sure wire terminals are clean and free from corrosion.

Installation

Reverse the *Removal* procedure to install the handlebar. Observe the following notes.

1. Be sure control cables are routed so that they will not be pinched at any position of the front end assembly.

2. Check cables for free movement.

3. Be sure wiring is connected properly.

4. Adjust clutch, front brake, and throttle cables after handlebar service. Refer to Chapter Two for procedures.

FORK TOP BRIDGE

The fork top bridge is mounted on top of the front fork assembly and is retained by the steering stem nut (**Figure 6**).

Removal

1. Remove the handlebar assembly (refer to *Handlebar, Removal*, preceding section).

2. Remove steering damper (if so equipped). See **Figure 7**.

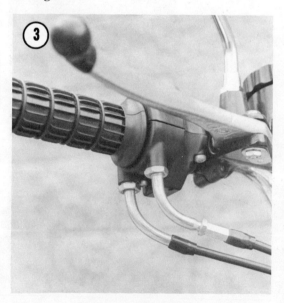

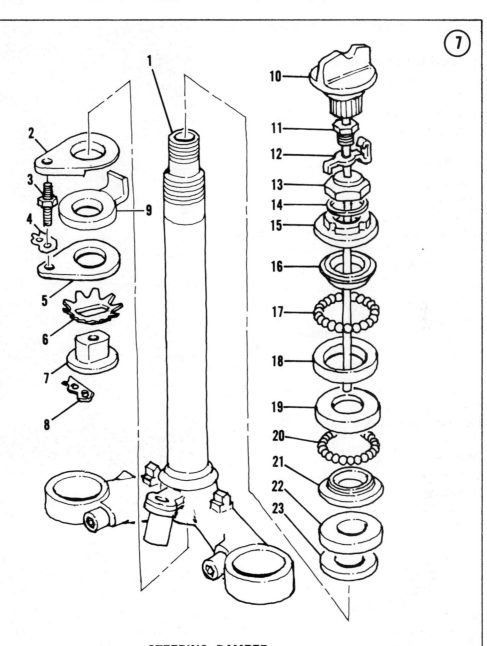

STEERING DAMPER

1. Steering stem
2. Steering damper plate A
3. Friction disc anchor bolt
4. Lock pin
5. Damper plate B
6. Steering damper spring
7. Steering damper nut
8. Lock pin
9. Damper friction disc
10. Steering head top thread
11. Damper lock spring set bolt
12. Damper lock spring
13. Steering stem nut
14. Steering stem washer
15. Steering head top thread
16. Top cone race
17. Steel ball
18. Top race
19. Bottom race
20. Steel ball
21. Bottom cone race
22. Steering head dust seal
23. Dust seal washer

3. Disconnect speedometer and tachometer cables (**Figure 8**).

4. Remove front fork top bolts and steering stem nut (**Figure 9**).

5. If so equipped, remove nuts, washers, cushions, and handlebar holders (**Figure 10**).

Inspection

Check for cracks or other damage, and replace worn cushions.

Installation

Reverse the *Removal* procedure, this section, to install the fork top bridge. Observe all notes under *Handlebar, Installation*, Steps 1-4.

STEERING STEM

The steering stem is supported by ball bearings at both ends which enable it to pivot in the frame headpipe (**Figure 11**). Most machines incorporate a steering damper.

Removal

1. Remove handlebar (refer to *Handlebar* section, this chapter).

2. Remove front wheel (refer to *Wheels* section, this chapter).

3. Remove both front fork legs (refer to *Front Fork* section, this chapter).

4. Remove front fork top bridge (refer to *Fork Top Bridge*, preceding section.

5. Remove steering stem nut (**Figure 12**), then carefully withdraw steering stem downward from frame headpipe (**Figure 13**).

> NOTE: *Be careful not to drop any steel balls.*

Inspection

Examine balls and races for cracks, chips, wear, or other damage. Be sure that dust seals are in good condition. Check for damaged threads. Refer to **Figure 14**.

> NOTE: *Never use any combination of new and used bearings. Replace bearings as complete sets if any defects are found.*

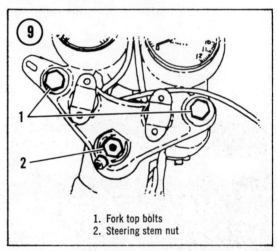

1. Fork top bolts
2. Steering stem nut

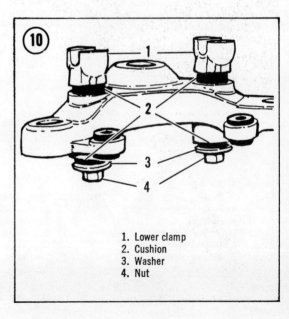

1. Lower clamp
2. Cushion
3. Washer
4. Nut

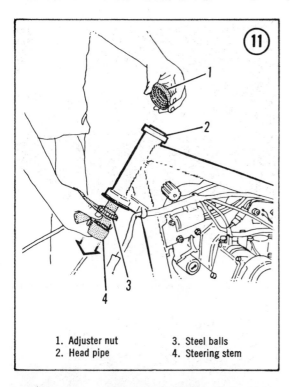

1. Adjuster nut   3. Steel balls
2. Head pipe   4. Steering stem

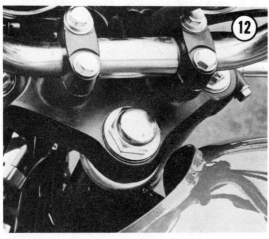

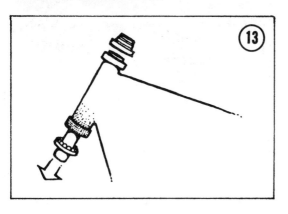

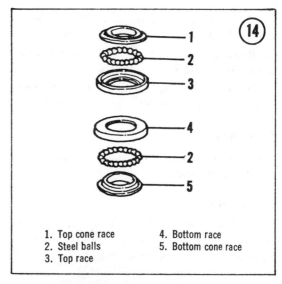

1. Top cone race   4. Bottom race
2. Steel balls   5. Bottom cone race
3. Top race

Installation

1. Clean bearings in solvent, then dry and lubricate thoroughly.

> NOTE: *Be careful not to drop any steel balls. Heavy grease will hold them during assembly.*

2. Insert the steering stem upward into the frame headpipe and thread the steering stem nut on. Tighten the nut enough so that the steering stem turns freely without looseness or binding. Refer to **Figure 12**.

WHEELS

Front Wheel Removal/Installation

1. Place a suitable stand under the frame so that the front wheel is off the ground.

2. Disconnect speedometer cable (**Figure 15**).

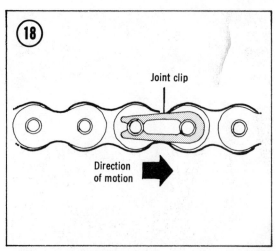

Joint clip

Direction
of motion

3. Remove fork cap nuts, then remove fork cap
(**Figure 16**).

4. Pull front wheel out (**Figure 17**).

5. Installation is the reverse of the preceding
steps.

Rear Wheel Removal/Installation

1. Remove master link and chain (**Figure 18**).

2. Remove wire safety clip on rear brake
torque link (**Figure 19**).

3. Remove nut and washer and remove rear
brake torque link (**Figure 20**).

4. On other side, remove cotter pin, axle nut,
and washer (**Figure 21**).

5. Remove brake adjusting nut and disconnect
brake cable (**Figure 22**).

6. Drive axle shaft out (**Figure 23**).

7. Pull wheel out to the rear (**Figure 24**).

8. To install rear wheel, perform the following steps:

   a. Insert wheel spacer (**Figure 25**).

   b. On other side, align axle and axle hole. Insert spacer and slide axle shaft in (grease it first). See **Figure 26**.

   c. Lightly tighten the axle nuts (**Figure 27**).

   d. Connect rear brake torque link with a washer and nut and install cotter pin (**Figure 28**).

   e. Install chain. Be sure master link is installed exactly as shown in **Figure 18**.

   f. Refer to **Figure 29**. Connect brake cable and thread brake adjusting nut on to rod. Turn each adjustment bolt (one on each side of wheel) until there is ¾-1 in. (20-25mm) of up and down movement in the center of the lower chain run (**Figure 30**).

7

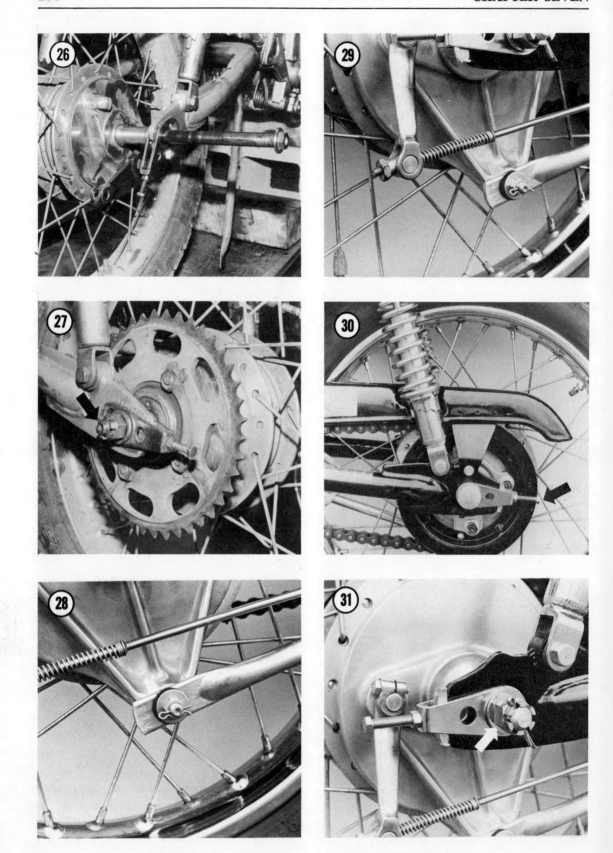

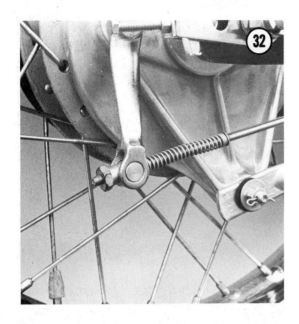

Tighten the locknuts (one on each side of wheel).

NOTE: *Be sure that the reference marks on the swinging arm and the index marks on the chain adjuster are in the same relative position on each side (refer to **Figure 29**).*

    g. Tighten the rear axle nuts and install new cotter pins (refer to **Figure 31**).

9. To adjust the rear brake, turn the adjusting nut (**Figure 32**) until the rear brake pedal has approximately ¾-1 in. (20-25mm) of free play (**Figure 33**).

Wheel Inspection

1. Refer to **Figure 34**. Mount the wheel so that a dial indicator can measure wheel rim runout. Observe the dial indicator while rotating the wheel. Runout limit for all models is 0.08 in. (2.0mm).

2. Check axles for bends by supporting the axle by its center in a V-block, then rotating the shaft. Measure runout at each end with dial indicators. Replace any axle which is bent more than 0.008 in. (0.2mm).

3. Check wheel bearings for cracks, galling, or pitting. Rotate them by hand to check for roughness. Replace bearings if they are worn or damaged. If bearings are satisfactory, clean them in solvent, dry thoroughly, and repack with fresh wheel bearing grease.

4. Check rear wheel shock absorbers for wear. Replace if worn or damaged.

5. Check spokes for looseness or bending. A bent or otherwise faulty spoke will affect neighboring ones, and should be replaced immediately. Refer to information under *Spokes*, later on in this section.

6. Inspect oil seals for wear or damage. Replace if there is any doubt about condition.

7. Check rims for bending or distortion.

Wheel Balance

    An unbalanced wheel results in unsafe riding conditions. Depending on the degree of unbalance and speed of the motorcycle, the rider may experience anything from a mild vibration to a

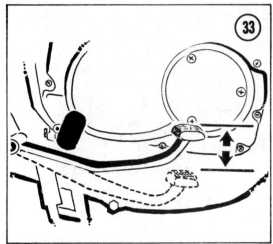

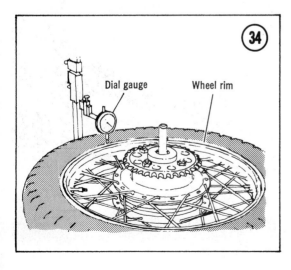

Dial gauge   Wheel rim

7

violent shimmy which may even result in loss of control. Balance weights may be installed to spokes on the light side of the wheel to correct this condition.

Before attempting to balance wheels, check to be sure that the wheel bearings are in good condition and properly lubricated. Also make sure that brakes don't drag, so that wheels rotate freely. With the wheel free of the ground, spin it slowly and allow it to come to rest by itself. Add balance weights to the spokes on the light side as required, so that the wheel comes to rest at a different position each time. Balance weights are available in weights of 10, 20, and 30 grams. Remove the drive chain before balancing rear wheels.

If more than one ounce is required to balance the wheel, add weight to adjacent spokes; never put two or more weights on the same spoke. When the wheel comes to rest at a different point each time the wheel is spun, consider it balanced and tightly crimp the weights so they won't be thrown off.

Spokes

Spokes should be checked for tightness. The "tuning fork" method of checking spoke tightness is simple and works well. Tap each spoke with a spoke wrench or shank of a screwdriver and listen to the tone. A tightened spoke will emit a clear, ringing tone, and a loose spoke will sound flat. All spokes in a correctly tightened wheel will emit tones of similar pitch but not necessarily the same precise tone.

Bent or stripped spokes should be replaced as soon as they are detected. Unscrew the nipple from the spoke and depress the nipple into the rim far enough to free the end of the spoke, taking care not to push the spoke all the way in. Remove the damaged spoke from the hub and use it to match a new spoke of identical length. If necessary, trim the new spoke to match the original and dress the end of the threads with a die. Install the new spoke in the hub and screw on the nipple, tightening it until the spoke's tone is similar to the tone of the other spokes on the wheel. Periodically check the new spoke; it will stretch and must be retightened several times before it takes its final set.

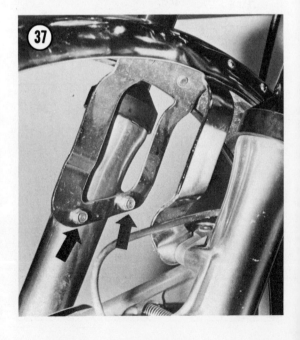

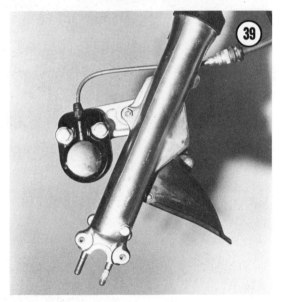

FRONT FORK

The front fork assembly serves as a shock absorber for the front wheel. Each leg consists of a spring and oil damper contained within telescoping tubes.

Removal

1. Place a pan under each fork leg, then remove drain plug at lower end of each fork leg and allow oil to drain out into pan (**Figure 35**).

> NOTE: *To aid in removing all of the oil, push down on the forks several times to force oil out.*

2. Remove front wheel (refer to *Wheels*, preceding section).

3. Remove headlight assembly (**Figure 36**).

4. Remove front fender bolts (**Figure 37**).

5. Disconnect hydraulic brake line from clip (**Figure 38**).

6. Remove fender (**Figure 39**).

7. Disconnect hydraulic brake line from brake caliper (**Figure 40**).

8. Remove brake caliper retaining bolts and remove caliper (**Figure 41**).

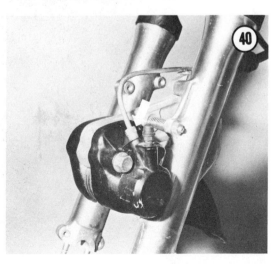

7

9. Remove plastic Honda name plate. See **Figures 42 and 43**.

10. Remove the top fork crown pinch bolts (**Figure 44**) and lower fork crown pinch bolts (**Figure 45**).

11. With a twisting motion, pull forks down and out (**Figure 46**).

Disassembly/Assembly

1. Remove top fork bolt (**Figure 47**).

2. Slide main spring out (**Figure 48**).

3. Remove rubber boot, then remove circlip with a pair of needle nose pliers (**Figure 49**).

4. Pry seal out (**Figure 50**).

5. Remove Allen screw at base of fork legs (**Figure 51**).

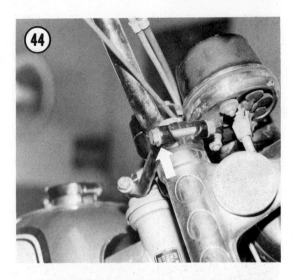

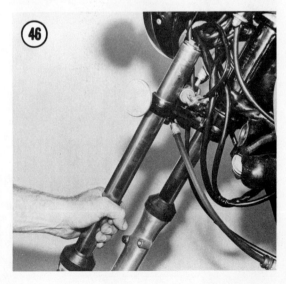

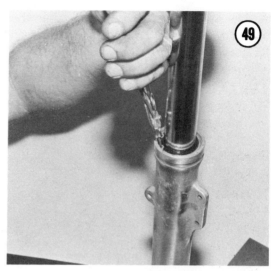

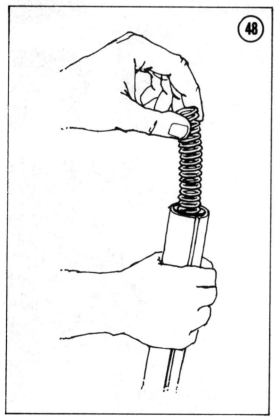

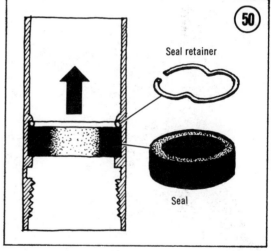

Seal retainer

Seal

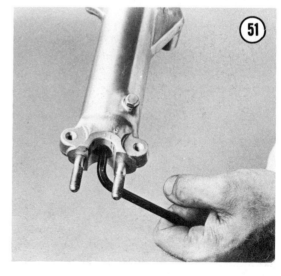

7

6. Place fork in a vise (use protective wood jaws or rags to prevent marring the fork) and pull fork apart (**Figure 52**).

7. To assemble, reverse preceding steps.

> NOTE: *Be sure that the oil seals are in good condition; replace if in doubt. Any roughness on the upper tube where it passes through the oil seal will cause rapid failure upon reassembly. To install the seal, press it into the fork with a suitable drift or proper size socket (Figure 53).*

Installation

1. Install the fork by reversing the steps listed under *Removal*, this section.

2. Fill the forks with fresh fork oil (refer to **Table 1**).

> NOTE: *When installing the front fender, the 2 long, gold colored bolts must go on the brake caliper side (they hold the brake caliper on, as well as the fender). See* **Figure 54**.

BRAKES

A disc brake is standard on the front, and a drum brake on the rear.

Disc Brake Caliper Removal

1. Remove the front wheel (refer to *Wheels* section, earlier in this chapter).

2. Disconnect hydraulic brake line from brake caliper (**Figure 55**).

3. Remove brake caliper retaining bolts and remove caliper (**Figure 56**).

Disc Brake Caliper Disassembly/Assembly

1. Disassemble caliper to the stage shown in **Figure 57**.

2. Remove bolts shown in **Figure 58** (hold caliper link in a vise).

3. Remove pin on back of the fixed brake pad and remove the pad (**Figure 59**). Check pad to be sure it is not worn to the red warning line. If it is, replace all pads in a set.

4. Remove the moveable pad (**Figure 60**). Check it for wear as in the previous step.

Table 1   FORK OIL QUANTITY

Model	Ounces	Cubic Centimeters
250 and 360	5.4-5.6	160-165

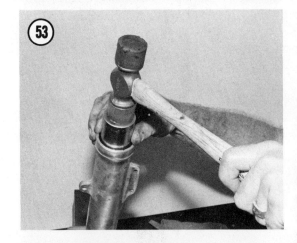

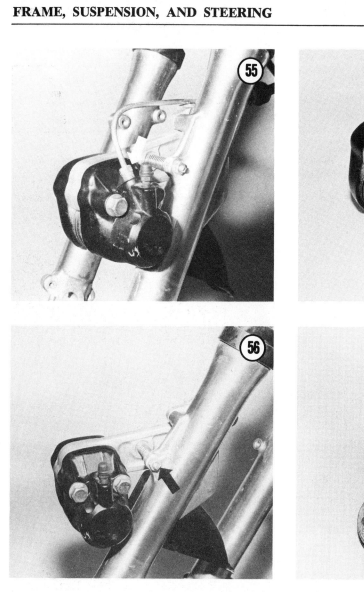

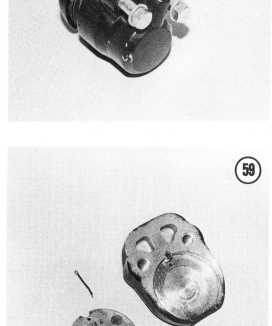

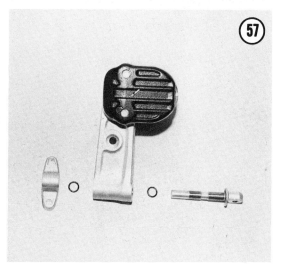

5. Install new pads and reassemble caliper by reversing the preceding steps.

Disc Brake
Caliper Installation

1. Install the brake caliper retaining bolts (refer to **Figure 56**).

2. Connect the hydraulic brake line to the caliper (refer to **Figure 55**).

3. Install the front wheel (refer to *Wheels* section, earlier in this chapter).

4. Bleed the hydraulic brake system (refer to *Brake Bleeding*, following section).

Brake Bleeding

The brake system must be bled any time air enters the system. Air may enter when the bleeder valve is open, or if the reservoir fluid level becomes too low.

1. Fill the brake fluid reservoir with fresh fluid (**Figure 61**). Check the level frequently during the bleeding procedure, as some fluid will be lost.

2. Remove the rubber cap from the bleeder valve, then connect a length of clear plastic tubing to the bleeder valve (**Figure 62**). Place the other end of the tube into a clean jar containing brake fluid. Be sure that the end of the tubing remains submerged in brake fluid during the entire procedure.

3. Open the bleeder valve, squeeze the brake lever slowly, close the valve, and release the lever. Repeat this sequence several times until the tube is full of fluid.

4. Open the bleeder valve. With the bleeder valve open, continue to slowly squeeze and

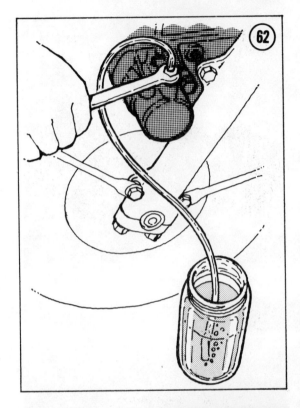

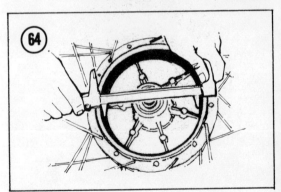

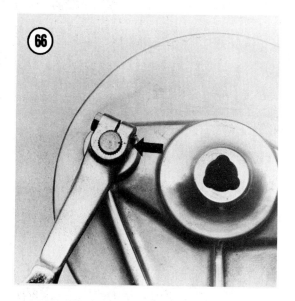

release the lever until no bubbles appear in either the brake fluid reservoir or in the fluid flowing from the bleeder valve. Add brake fluid to the reservoir as necessary to maintain the proper level.

5. Close the bleeder valve, replace the rubber cap, and fill the resevoir to the line (refer to **Figure 61**).

Drum Brake
Removal/Installation

1. Remove rear wheel (refer to *Wheels* section, earlier in this chapter).

2. Pull brake assembly out as shown in **Figure 63**.

3. Measure the brake drum inner diameter with a vernier caliper (**Figure 64**). Replace if brake drum is worn beyond service limits recommended in **Table 2**. Also measure brake lining thickness and replace if worn to less than the wear limits specified in **Table 3**.

4. To replace brake shoes, refer to **Figure 65**. Remove the cotter pin, washer, springs, and brake shoes. Reverse disassembly procedure to reassemble the brake assembly.

> NOTE: *If brake arms have been removed, be sure that the punch marks on the brake arm align with corresponding mark on brake cam (**Figure 66**).*

5. **Figure 67** shows the brake completely assembled from the front; **Figure 68** from the back.

Table 2   BRAKE DRUM SERVICE LIMITS

Model	Service Limits	
	Inches	Millimeters
250 and 360		
Front	7.17	182
Rear	6.38	162

Table 3   BRAKE LINING WEAR LIMITS

Model	Inches	Millimeters
250 and 360		
Front	0.12	3.0
Rear	0.12	3.0

7

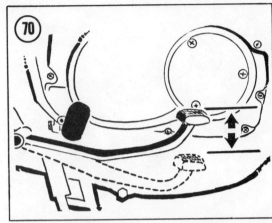

6. Reverse Steps 1 and 2, preceding, to install the brake assembly and rear wheel.

Front Disc Brake Adjustment

The front disc brake is self-adjusting.

Rear Drum Brake Adjustment

The rear drum brake is operated by a rod. Simply turn the adjusting nut (**Figure 69**) until the rear brake pedal has approximately ¾-1 in. (20-25mm) of free play (**Figure 70**).

REAR SUSPENSION

The major rear suspension components are two shock absorbers, two springs, and a swinging arm.

Shock Absorbers and Springs

The rear shock absorbers are not serviceable, and must be replaced in the event of malfunction, as follows.

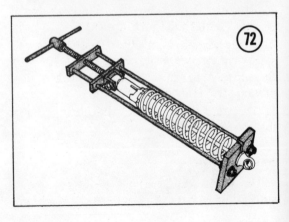

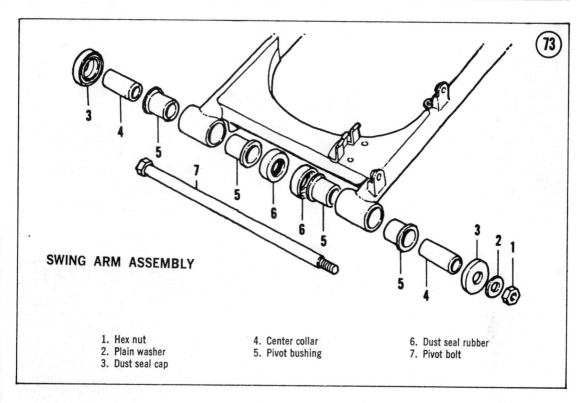

SWING ARM ASSEMBLY

1. Hex nut
2. Plain washer
3. Dust seal cap
4. Center collar
5. Pivot bushing
6. Dust seal rubber
7. Pivot bolt

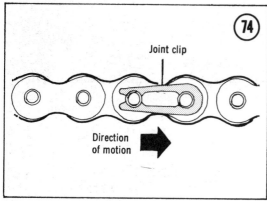

Joint clip

Direction
of motion

1. Remove shock absorber mounting bolts (**Figure 71**) and pull shock absorbers off.

2. Compress the shock absorber with a special spring compressor as shown in **Figure 72**, until the spring seat can be removed. Then release pressure from the tool.

3. To install the new shock absorbers, reverse the preceding steps.

Swinging Arm

The pivot section of the swinging arm is susceptible to wear, especially in the shaft and bushings. Replace the pivot shaft if it is bent more than 0.02 in. (0.5mm). Replace bushings and/or shaft if the clearance between them exceeds 0.014 in. (0.35mm).

Disassemble the swinging arm and grease its pivot shaft and bushings every 6,000 miles (9,000 kilometers). Refer to **Figure 73** for the following procedure:

1. Remove hex nut, washer, and dust seal cap.

2. Slide pivot bolt out of center collar.

3. Remove center collar. Grease inside of the pivot bush; inside and outside of center collar; and outside of pivot bolt.

4. Reassemble by reversing the preceding steps.

DRIVE CHAIN

The drive chain becomes worn after prolonged use. Wear in pins, bushings, and rollers causes chain stretch. Sliding action between roller surfaces and sprocket teeth also contribute to wear.

Cleaning and Adjustment

1. Disconnect the master link (**Figure 74**) and remove chain.

7

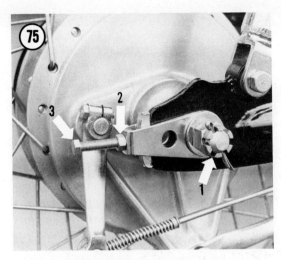

1. Rear axle nut   2. Locknut
3. Adjustment bolt

2. Clean chain thoroughly in solvent.

3. Rinse chain with clean solvent, then blow dry with compressed air.

4. Examine chain carefully for wear or damage. Replace if there is any doubt as to its condition. If chain is OK, lubricate by soaking in oil, or any of the special chain lubricants available in any motorcycle shop.

5. Install the chain. Be sure that the master link is installed as shown in **Figure 74**.

6. Refer to **Figure 75**. Adjust chain as follows:

a. Remove cotter pin and loosen rear axle nut.

b. Loosen locknut on each side.

c. There is one adjustment bolt on each side. Turn it until there is ¾-1 in. (20-25mm) of up and down movement in the center of the lower chain run (**Figure 76**).

d. Be sure that the reference marks on the swinging arm and the index mark on the chain adjuster (refer to **Figure 75**) are in the same relative positions on each side.

7. Tighten the rear axle nut, then install a new cotter pin (refer to **Figure 75**).

8. Adjust the rear brake (refer to *Brake Adjustment*, this chapter).

CHAPTER EIGHT

PERFORMANCE IMPROVEMENT

The Honda 360 twin was more than a slightly larger-engined replacement for the 350 (actually 325cc's) series of Hondas.

The 350 was designed and sold as a general purpose motorcycle, intended for every use from around-town and medium-distance touring to dirt riding.

However, with increased sophistication both in the available machinery and in motorcycle rider/buyers, the idea of the universal motorcycle became obsolete.

When the 360 replaced the 350, it was with the idea that the new machine would be a "utility" bike; intended for use as a first full-size or commuter machine, providing acceptable street and freeway performance at a moderate cost with high reliability and relatively inexpensive parts and maintenance costs.

But for many riders, familiarity and experience means a desire for more performance. There are many good reasons to want more performance. The bike may be intended for use as a touring motorcycle, and will need more horsepower to carry the added load of traveling gear plus a companion. More street performance will give improved passing and acceleration times. Better handling will improve general riding and increase capabilities on mountain roads.

Moderate improvements in all these areas may be made to the 360. However, the 360 cannot be turned into a firebreathing superbike without the expenditure of massive amounts of money and a great deal of custom building.

Nor is the 360 suitable for any kind of competition use. No matter how much money is spent, the 360 cannot be competitive with the extremely sophisticated competition-oriented bikes of today.

Owners who want significantly greater performance should trade up to a larger bike rather than sink a fortune into their 360's. A larger bike, such as the Honda 550 or 750 Four, would be a far more economical and reliable step than a super-hot-rodded 360, which will have the reliability of a hand grenade — and still less performance than either of the above-mentioned stock motorcycles.

By far the most sensible way to go performance is step-by-step. First, you can maintain a budget, by setting aside money each month for each stage of performance building. Secondly, each performance boost can be added at the right time, to gain optimum benefit from previous improvement. Thirdly, each improvement may be dialed in, until it provides the maximum benefit. When several changes are made at once, it can be difficult to make

sure each new component is performing at maximum efficiency. Finally, step-by-step building
ensures that the bike will not be overbuilt with
performance (or maintenance requirements) beyond what the owner wants or is willing to
provide.

Performance manufacturers are listed in
Table 1, found at the end of the chapter.

HANDLING

The Honda 360 twin cannot be described as
anything other than a mediocre handling
motorcycle. While minor improvement is possible, major improvement is not.

The handling limitations are ultimately trace-
able to the 360's frame. Some experimentation
might be done with gusseting the frame tubing
at potential flex areas, although no research has
been done in this particular area. Merely
welding plates on a frame is no guarantee that
improvements will result, and any work in this
area should be done only by experienced,
competition-minded builders.

It would also be possible to replace the stock
frame with a custom-built frame from C&J —
but very few riders are willing to spend well
over $600 on a Honda 360, and still be left with
the necessity of adding all necessary mounting
tabs and hardware to mount components required for street use of a motorcycle.

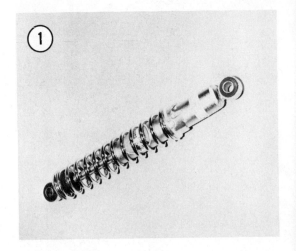

Shocks

Replacement of the marginal rear shocks on
the 360 twin can significantly improve handling
characteristics. Stock shock absorbers are
undersprung, lack adequate damping, and wear
out rapidly. Any motorcycle with over 5,000
miles on it almost certainly has wornout shock
absorbers.

Rather than using stock replacements, accessory performance shocks should be used.
Conventional spring-oil damping shocks from
high-quality manufacturers such as S&W,
Koni, or Number One (**Figure 1**) are recommended.

One of the best sets of shocks available is
from S&W, which is available with either single
rate or progressive rate springs. For solo street
riding, use 70-110 lb. progressive rate

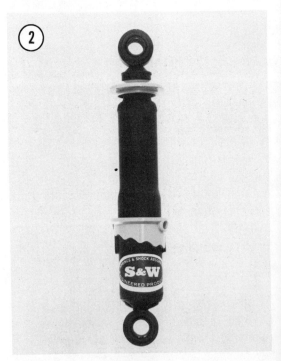

springs. For two-up street riding, use 85-115 lb.
progressives. If the bike is used for touring, try
62-95 lb. springs for solo and 85-115 lb. for
two-up.

These will not only provide the correct spring
rate for motorcycle and rider, but far more
exact damping, as well as a lifespan well in excess of 40,000 miles.

More expensive, but better suited for the
rider who wants better control, are S&W airshocks or Number One Products hydraulic
shocks. Either can be set for the proper ride

height with widely varying loads or heavily pre-loaded for precision handling.

Airshocks (**Figure 2**) replace the standard spring with an air reservoir. This reservoir is pumped to whatever pressure is desired to regulate the springing. Damping is handled by a conventional oil system, and can be adjusted to some extent by varying the amount of oil in the shocks. These shocks are available either with a handlebar-mounted pressure gauge and air pressure line, or a simpler setup with a T-fitting, mounted under the seat, with lines connected to the shocks. The airshocks are available with an optional syringe-pump, so that pressure may be adjusted without having to use a gas station airhose.

The Number One hydraulic shocks have a remote-mounted hydraulic reservoir. Fluid may be fed from the reservoir into the shocks to adjust the ride height. Shock control is through a handlebar-mounted lever, much like a small clutch lever, and a pressure gauge. A backup spring is mounted inside the shock, so that if hydraulic pressure is lost, the rider will still be able to keep riding.

With either of these shocks the owner may avoid the trap of single-purpose equipment — installing a component which does one thing very well, but makes the machine less suitable for all-around conditions.

Swing Arm

A second factor in imprecise handling frequently is swing arm bushing wear. Since the

360 twin uses synthetic or plain bronze bushings, these should be checked frequently for wear.

Remove the rear wheel and shocks, and move the swing arm from side to side. If there is *any* appreciable side play, remove the swing arm and check the pivot shaft/bushing clearance (it should be no more than 0.35mm maximum). The pivot bolt should also be checked to see if it is bent or worn; if so, replace it.

The stock bushings should be replaced with a set of oilite bronze bushings from Pro Tec (**Figure 3**). These bushings not only have far greater life expectancy than the stockers, but also provide closer pivot bolt/bushing tolerance and consequently less swing arm side play.

Front Forks

Another problem area in handling is the stock front forks. Their problems are several: they are insufficiently sprung, the damping rod assembly is inadequate, and they are easily distorted by side stresses incurred during braking/acceleration/cornering.

However, before modifying the front forks to cure a problem, make sure that the swing arm bushings are in good condition and the steering head bearings are in good condition and properly adjusted.

Normally, a utility machine such as the 360 twin is given utility maintenance — what goes visibly wrong gets fixed. Since the steering head bearings are out of sight, quite frequently they are allowed to go square, out-of-round and unlubricated.

To check the bearings, remove the front forks and disassemble the steering stem as described in Chapter Seven. Clean the top and bottom races and examine them closely for wear. If worn, replace them.

No performance damping rod assembly kits exist, however some improvement in damping is possible by replacing the stock 20-weight oil with Bel Ray 30-weight fork oil.

The tendency of the forks to tweak under sideload may be reduced by installing a Circle Industries' fork brace (**Figure 4**).

Even with the outlined improvements, the stock front forks are still barely adequate for high performance riding conditions.

8

Major improvement requires replacing the stockers with a set of 38mm Ceriani roadracing forks, at considerable expense. These forks will require fabrication of brackets to mount headlight, gauges, handlebars, etc., and the stock front fender must be replaced with a clamp-on cafe racer type fender such as those available from Dick's Cycle West.

Even with the addition of the Cerianis, the frame limitations of the 360 will mean that the bike still handles only moderately well.

Wheels

Reduction of unsprung weight (that portion of the motorcycle acted on directly by the road surface, such as wheels, tires, brakes, lower fork legs, etc. — see **Figure 5**) will also improve handling.

The stock rims may be replaced with a set of lightweight Akront or DID rims. However, this does little to cut the major cause of the Honda's extremely heavy wheel weight — the massive hub/brake assemblies.

For a considerable investment (over $300), the stock wheels may be replaced with a set of Morris Industries' cast alloy wheels **(Figure 6)**. Since there have been few orders for these set up for 360's, there is an additional charge for custom setup.

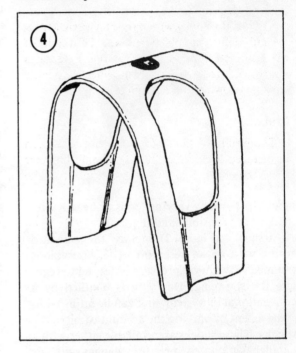

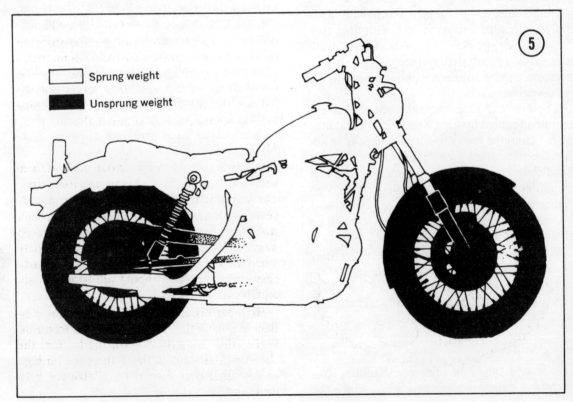

Sprung weight

Unsprung weight

Cast aluminum alloy wheels must be coupled with an accessory rear disc brake assembly and an accessory rear sprocket, such as the lightweight alloy item available from Circle Industries (**Figure 7**).

The weight saving with a set of Morris wheels is significant. Completely set up, the weight of the complete rear wheel assembly is reduced almost 20 pounds and front wheel assembly weight is down about 3 pounds.

Brakes

The weight of the stock front disc brake can be reduced by drilling the disc. Small diameter holes are drilled in offset locations and the

holes are countersunk slightly on each side to prevent excessive puck wear. The holes also improve braking in wet weather. Since the stock discs are extremely difficult to work with, it is recommended that this modification be performed by an experienced motorcycle performance shop (such as Bill Bowman, Inc., for around $30 per disc).

Some riders have attempted to reduce rear wheel weight by drilling holes in the brake backing plate. This is extremely hazardous, since it structurally weakens the hub to the point of failure. Hole drilling will also completely remove any water resistant capabilities that the stock hub has, and guarantee complete loss of rear brakes in wet weather.

Several accessory disc brake systems are available for use on the rear wheel. The Italian-built Grimeca is the most suitable. It's more efficient (styled much like the super-expensive Lockheed brake system), and no more expensive than most other systems available.

The Grimeca (or Lockheed or Hurst/Airheart) systems are available either as component parts from Morris Industries, or custom designed for your motorcycle by Performance Machine.

It should be emphasized that the use of a rear disc brake will not significantly affect stopping distance. Approximately 60-70% of a motorcycle's braking efficiency is controlled by the front brake — the rear brake serves only to balance the front brake and prevent the bike from swapping ends under braking.

Tires

When the stock tires wear out, replace them with a set of high performance street tires. Those manufactured by Continental, Goodyear, or Dunlop give far better adhesion than stock tires at the expense of slightly increased wear. However, since the Honda 360 has only moderate horsepower, and is not a particularly heavy bike, tire wear should still be within acceptable limits.

High-performance builders should not consider changing the rear wheel to a 16 inch rim. While this is stylish (particularly for the chopper-oriented modifiers), there are no high performance tires currently available for a 16 inch rim.

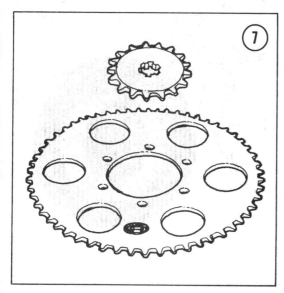

8

Engine

Since the stock Honda 360 twin is not highly stressed, it accepts a fairly great increase in horsepower without being overbuilt.

None of the commonly available modifications require disassembly of the engine beyond removal of the top end, so downtime is minimal. These modifications, in addition to increasing performance, will also make the bike more efficient and pleasant to ride.

Exhaust

Three considerations are made by Honda engineers when designing their exhaust systems, each integrated with the other. The system must be efficient, meet the current noise emission standards, and be as economical as possible.

While the stock systems are reasonably efficient, they are certainly not the *most* efficient for the performance enthusiast. Also, stock Honda exhausts have always been known for collecting internal moisture which rust out the pipes. For these reasons, plus styling, most riders will replace their 360's exhaust during the time they own the bike.

While all bike owners want the maximum power from their exhaust systems, too many of them confuse increased noise with increased performance. A louder bike is not automatically faster. The common practice of gutting the stock mufflers, or (worse yet) removing the mufflers and running with open pipes, is more likely to produce less power and possible engine damage than increased performance.

CAUTION
Under no circumstances should a motorcycle ever be run with open (un-muffled) exhausts. This is not only illegal, but makes a black mark for all motorcyclists, which may result in still further and more stringent anti-motorcycle legislation.

Far too many accessory exhaust systems are no more functional then gutted-out stockers. They may be better looking than the stock pipes, but are far less efficient.

A power-producing exhaust that still maintains acceptable noise output is the downsweep header system, muffled by two wide-diameter glasspacks. Excellent systems of this type are available from Drag Specialties and Hooker Headers (**Figure 8**).

A second type of high-performance system is the two-into-one system from either Hooker or Drag Specialties. With this style exhaust, the left header pipe crosses to join the right header, and both enter a common muffler on the right side of the bike.

Any exhaust system which makes the engine breathe better requires carburetor rejetting. Few benefits are gained without this very important stage in building. In fact, rejetting is

usually necessary any time a performance change is made to any part of the engine.

Better breathing makes an engine run leaner than before, therefore it is often necessary to increase the carburetor main jet by one size or more. Performing a plug chop as described below is the only way to tell. Since Hondas have a tendency to come jetted one or two sizes too rich stock (a precautionary measure taken to prevent the engine from running too lean, and possibly seizing), don't be surprised if rejetting is not necessary.

The first step in carburetor jetting is to take a high-speed plug chop: Run the bike in any gear above 4,000 rpm for ⅛-¼ mile. Cut the ignition switch pull in the clutch and allow the bike to drift to a halt. Remove the plugs and examine them (**Figure 9**, page 124). Correct the carburetor jetting accordingly.

Normally, the only change which should be necessary when installing a hot rod exhaust system is to the main jet. However, if there is any hesitation on acceleration, the jet needle clip may need to be lowered one notch.

Big Bore Kit

The biggest and most noticeable performance improvement comes from increasing the displacement. A big bore kit from a reputable manufacturer will produce significantly greater horsepower, without making the engine peaky, cammy, or unreliable. Obviously, increasing an engine's displacement will also slightly decrease its fuel economy.

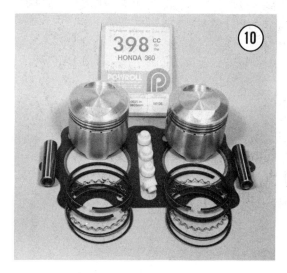

For the Honda 360, two big bore kits are available from Powroll Performance Products. They consist of new cast pistons, rings, piston pins and retainers, and head gasket. They increase the engine displacement to 398cc's (**Figure 10**).

Installation requires removal of the head and cylinder. The stock cylinder liners must be bored to accommodate the new 70.75mm pistons. This work may be done by any competent automotive or motorcycle machine shop, or by mail by Powroll for a cost of around $30.

The two kits differ in one significant way: the compression ratio. The basic kit ups compression to 9.1:1, and is the only kit recommended for street use.

The second kit, built for the competition rider, increases compression to 12.5:1. The higher compression ratio will slightly increase torque, but at the expense of increased engine heat, wear, and strain. Also, compression ratios over 10:1 require the finest of high-premium gas — something which is generally unavailable at normal gas stations. Since it is very hard to make the Honda 360 competitive in today's sophisticated competition scene, the high-compression kit is not really recommended under any circumstances.

With a big bore kit installed, use a 20-50 weight multigrade oil in the crankcase, preferably from a super-quality manufacturer such as Kendall, Castrol, or Valvoline.

Care should also be taken to watch the redline — higher displacement increases engine strain. While the stock 360 may be blithely overrevved without damage, the possiblities of breakage are significantly increased with a high performance engine.

Camshaft

With a big bore kit installed, further improvements are possible by replacing the stock cam with a Powroll Performance cam shaft (**Figure 11**). Like almost all cams made for non-superbikes, the Powroll cam is a hardweld. That is, the lobes on a stock cam are built up with welding material, then the surface is ground to the new profile. Finally, the shaft is hardened.

Novice motorcycle performance builders may be familiar with automotive terms to

8

Normal plug appearance noted by the brown to grayish-tan deposits and slight electrode wear. This plug indicates the correct plug heat range and proper air fuel ratio.

Red, brown, yellow and white coatings caused by fuel and oil additives. These deposits are not harmful if they remain in a powdery form.

Carbon fouling distinguished by dry, fluffy black carbon deposits which may be caused by an over-rich air/fuel mixture, excessive hand choking, clogged air filter or excessive idling.

Shiny yellow glaze on insulator cone is caused when the powdery deposits from fuel and oil additives melt. Melting occurs during hard acceleration after prolonged idling. This glaze conducts electricity and shorts out the plug.

Oil fouling indicated by wet, oily deposits caused by oil pumping past worn rings or down the intake valve guides. A hotter plug temporarily reduces oil deposits, but a plug that is too hot leads to pre-ignition and possible engine damage.

Overheated plug indicated by burned or blistered insulator tip and badly worn electrodes. This condition may be caused by pre-ignition, cooling system defects, lean air/fuel ratios, low octane fuel or over advanced ignition timing.

Spark plug condition photos courtesy of AC Spark Plug Division, General Motors Corporation.

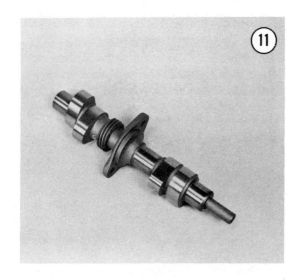

describe camshafts — "three-quarter race," "full race," etc. Motorcycle cams are more often described in terms of their potential use: "street," "hillclimb," "roadrace," "drag-race," etc. Care must be taken not to pick too hot a cam for a motorcycle — a car can be run with a fairly radical cam and be more liveable on the street than a motorcycle equivalently equipped. Normally the ideal cam for street use is one with moderately increased lift and duration, rather than a super-radical, high-lift, road-racing design.

The Powroll cam is just right for the street; it increases intake opening and closing to 13/55 degrees, exhaust to 55/15. Valve lift is 0.380 inch.

Used in a stock engine, low end performance is slightly less than stock, with a significant increase from 6-11,000 rpm. However, when this cam is coupled with the 398cc big bore kit, bottom end performance is better than stock, and the gains between 6-11,000 rpm are very noticeable. (Powroll charts give an increase from stock of 4 hp at 9000 rpm.)

Since this camshaft is moderate in design, no modification to the head need be made on installation. The only non-stock accessory which must be used with the camshaft is a set of heavy-duty Powroll valve springs to avoid coil-bind and possible valve train failure.

If this cam is installed on a stock engine, the valve pockets on the piston must be deepened, to allow for the increased valve travel. This service may be performed by mail order to Pow-

roll and the pistons should accompany the cam order.

If installed in conjunction with the 398 kit, the Powroll pistons are already set up to allow for the increased valve travel and will require no modification.

Other camshafts are available for the 360, most of them having approximately the same configuration as the Powroll. However, whenever possible, all engine components should be ordered from the same manufacturer. Builders who use a cam from one manufacturer, valve springs from a second, and a big bore kit from a third may find a fair amount of difficulty in amalgamating these components into a smooth-running, optimum engine.

If a different camshaft is used with the 398 kit, or if stock pistons are used, piston/valve clearance must be checked carefully. This may be done in the old style, by putting the engine together with a layer of modelling clay atop each piston, turning the engine through, removing the head, and measuring the indentations in the clay. However, this is not only involved and messy, but the inexperienced builder may allow bits of clay to fall into the engine's lower end. Unretrieved, these will quickly cause engine failure.

A far simpler, yet accurate, method is described below. First remove the cylinder head and disassemble the valve train as described in Chapter Four.

1. Remove the alternator cover, and install a degree wheel on the engine.

2. Turn the engine through until piston No. 1 is at top dead center (TDC). Position a pointer (wire, coat hanger, etc.) so that it points to 0 degrees on the degree wheel.

3. Reassemble the valve train into the head, using a weak spring (carb slide spring, door-spring, etc.) of the same diameter and in place of the valve springs. Do not install the camshaft, rocker arms, etc.

4. Install the head on the engine.

5. Position a dial indicator gauge on the head (magnetic mounts are available at auto parts stores) so that the pointer tip rests on cylinder No. 1 intake valve stem, and the pointer will travel in approximately the same direction as the valve.

8

6. Zero the dial indicator gauge. Depress the valve until it touches the top of the piston. Read the amount of travel on the dial indicator.

7. Turn the engine through to 10 degrees after top dead center (ATDC), repeating Step 6 every few degrees.

8. Write down the *minimum* figure reached in Steps 6 and 7.

CAUTION
On some bikes actual top dead center of the piston may occur at a different point than the TDC *mark.*

9. Consult the camshaft manufacturer's specifications to determine valve lift. Some manufacturers state total valve lift beginning with the valve fully seated. Others state valve lift beginning with the valve partially open. If the valve is partially open, you must add this amount to the specified valve lift to determine actual total valve lift. In order to provide adequate clearance between valve and piston, you must also add 0.060 in. as a safety margin.

NOTE: *Here is an example of the calculation. Powroll's #12675 camshaft has a specified valve lift of 0.380 in. This is measured with the valve 0.040 in. off its seat. Therefore, the **total** lift is 0.420 in. Add 0.060 in. safety margin and 0.480 in. clearance is required.*

10. Compare the necessary clearance calculated in Step 9 to the actual measured clearance in Step 8. If actual clearance is less than calculated clearance, the valve pocket in the piston must be cut deeper.

11. Turn the engine through until cylinder No. 1 is at 10 degrees before top dead center (BTDC).

12. Install the dial indicator gauge on cylinder No. 1 exhaust valve stem, and repeat Step 5.

13. Turn the engine through to TDC, repeating the measuring procedure as in Step 7. Again, write down the *minimum* figure reached.

14. Again, use the manufacturer's specifications to calculate total valve lift by adding specified valve lift to the amount that the valve is off its seat when valve lift is measured. Add 0.100 in. clearance as a safety margin.

15. The calculated clearance in Step 13 must be greater than the actual measured clearance in Step 14. If not, then the exhaust valve pocket on the piston must be cut deeper.

16. If a deeper cut is not required, remove the head, remove the keeper and weak spring, and continue normal reassembly of the engine from that point.

Valve Train

Various exotic modifications to the valve train have been performed, such as offset rocker arms, lightened assembly, etc. None of these are of benefit for street use, and all of them weaken components.

The only modification which might be considered to the valve train would be use of high-quality bronze guides, to replace the stock parts. Performance is not increased, but valve train lifespan will be somewhat greater.

Carburetion

The constant-vacuum carburetors used on the 360 Honda have a number of virtues, including reliability, consistency of performance, ease of adjustment, and lack of temperament. Also, at least in theory, their ability to match flow rate to engine requirements means that they should be ideal for performance.

However, CV carburetors tend to have a fairly limited flow rate, and their lack of immediate response to acceleration changes means that for the performance rider they are less than ideal and should be replaced.

The ideal replacements are two Mikuni slide/needle carburetors. Use 28mm venturi carburetors on a stock or near-stock engine, and 30mm venturi carburetors on a bike with a big bore kit.

These carburetors may be ordered from Powroll Performance, for around $200 ready to mount on your engine. When ordering, specify your riding attitude, style of riding, and what modifications, if any, are done to the bike (exhaust, cams, big bore, etc.).

When shipped, the carburetors will be closely pre-jetted, slightly richer than ideal. The only modifications necessary should be to the main jet size, jet needle clip position, and possibly the air jet.

It should be emphasized that these carburetors should be ordered pre-jetted. Too many riders find an old Mikuni, attached to a junked dirt bike, and decide they're going to set the carburetor up for their own, vastly different, machines.

Unless someone in this position is an extremely experienced carburetor tuner, he is almost certainly doomed to failure — the Mikuni has more possible jetting combinations than the super-complex Weber. Correct jetting will not only mean buying a wide assortment of jets (generally around $1 each), but a selection of slides as well (at around $5 each).

The stock air cleaner box and element should be removed, and Uni or K&N air filters used. Mount the air filters directly to the carburetor bellmouths.

Velocity stacks, so-called airhorns, are not recommended for use on the street, due to the possibility of drawing dirt and debris directly into the engine.

Headwork

Even with more efficient carburetion, the mixture flow may still be markedly improved by porting.

Basic head porting consists of smoothing the intake and exhaust ports, improving the contour of the ports, removing restrictions to the intake/exhaust flow, and ensuring that both combustion chambers are equal in volume.

This is one area of performance improvement where there are nothing but gains — performance and fuel economy are increased 10-15% without affecting reliability.

While the work may appear to be simple, it is not to be done by an inexperienced worker. Experimenting on your cylinder head with a Dremel tool is more likely to produce an expensive ashtray than improved performance.

Headwork should only be done by an experienced motorcycle head porting service. Even automotive porters should be avoided — the degree of tolerance and hence, mistakes allowable on a V-8 head is infinitely more than that on a small displacement 2-cylinder motorcycle like the 360.

One of Powroll Performance's specialties is headwork on Honda twins. For a moderate price (around $150), they guarantee a minimum flow improvement of 8% on the intake ports and 18% on the exhaust ports.

After porting, the carburetors require rejetting. The rider who doesn't feel that he has the resources or experience for this might be best advised to order his replacement carburetors at the same time he sends the head to Powroll for porting.

It must be emphasized that porting must be accompanied by a complete and skillful valve job, and the replacement of any worn or unserviceable components.

ELECTRICAL

The final stage in engine modification should be to the ignition system. Honda's ignition has never been considered more than adequate. Most Hondas are susceptible to points bounce at high rpm, causing erratic firing and consequent loss of power.

No bolt-on high-performance ignition system, such as a magneto, distributor, or CDI, exists for the Honda 360. The rider interested in maximum performance at high rpm may use a double set of springs on his points. The reduction of points bounce will, of course, be coupled with an increased wear on the points and points cam.

The stock coil, which is generally rated at around 10,000 volts output, should be replaced, with either 2 automotive coils (those available from K-Mart discount stores are both high output and very inexpensive) or a single dual-wire coil from Andrews Products. This coil is rated at 30,000 volts output and will provide noticeably improved performance.

The stock plug wires should be replaced with Thundervolt wires, available from Drag Specialties.

A frequent cause of electrical breakdowns on Honda 360's, particularly the earlier models, can be traced to regulator failure. The entire regulatory system may be replaced with a solid-state Sebring Power Pack, for improved reliability. The Pack, a small finned metal box, may be easily mounted in place of the stock components.

CLUTCH & GEARING

Since the stock Honda 360 clutch is not particularly strong, it should be replaced, when

8

worn out, with a set of plates from Barnett Tool & Engineering. This replacement kit will not only give better hookup, but significantly increased life.

High-performance engines, particularly those used in off-the-line riding, should have Barnett heavy-duty clutch springs used in place of the stockers.

While these springs do increase clutch actuating pressure, they will also guarantee there will be no clutch slipping. Both clutch pack and springs are drop-in replacement items.

Gearing may be modified by custom-ordering a countershaft or rear sprocket from Circle Industries. In addition to giving precisely the gearing needed, the Circle sprockets last for an extremely long time and reduce unsprung weight on the rear wheel.

OVERALL

While the Honda 360 twin will never be considered a superbike, it takes very kindly to a moderate amount of high performance increase. With suspension and braking improved to match more engine power, the Honda twin is not only faster and quicker, but far safer and more reliable to ride — a worthwhile goal for any engine builder/rider, performance oriented or not.

Table 1   SOURCES

Manufacturer	Services
Andrews Products, Inc. 9872 Farragut St. Rosemont, Ill. 60018	High-output coils
Barnett Tool & Engineering 4915 Pacific Blvd. Vernon, Ca. 90058	Heavy duty clutch kits
Bill Bowman, Inc. 2546 Manhattan Ave. Montrose, Ca. 91020	Disc brake lightening
C & J Precision Products 1151 E. Mission Fallbrook, Ca. 92028	Custom frames
Circle Industries 17901 Arenth Ave. Industry, Ca. 91749	Sprockets, fork braces
Dick's Cycle West 304 Agostino Road San Gabriel, Ca. 91776	Fiberglass fenders
Drag Specialties 6868 Washington Ave. So. Eden Prairie, Minn. 55343	Exhaust, ignition wiring kits
Hooker Headers P.O. Box 4090 Ontario, Ca. 91761	Exhaust pipes
Morris Industries 2901 W. Garry Ave. Santa Ana, Ca. 92704	Cast alloy wheels, disc brake components
Number One Products 4931 N. Encinita Ave. Temple City, Ca. 91780	Shocks, fork springs, damping kits
Performance Machine 16248 Minnesota Paramount, Ca. 90723	Disc brake systems
Powroll Performance Products P.O. Box 1206 Bend, Ore. 97701	High performance engine components, porting, engine machining
S&W Engineered Products 2616 W. Woodland Dr. Anaheim, Ca. 92801	Shocks, fork springs
Sebring Electronics 8852 Lower River Road Grants Pass, Ore. 97526	Power converter

8

INDEX

MAINTENANCE LOG

DATE	TYPE OF SERVICE	COST	REMARKS

NOTES

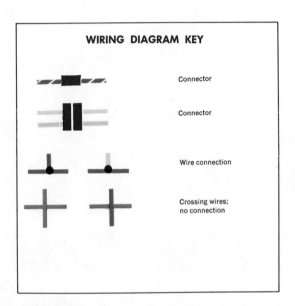

WIRING DIAGRAM KEY

Connector

Connector

Wire connection

Crossing wires;
no connection